HOW TO BE A
Genius

Chris Garratt,
Mick Kidd
and David Stafford

Methuen

First published in Great Britain 1994
by Methuen London
an imprint of Reed Consumer Books Ltd
Michelin House, 81 Fulham Road, London SW3 6RB
and Auckland, Melbourne, Singapore and Toronto

A CIP catalogue record for this book
is available at the British Library
ISBN 0 413 68710 4

Typeset by Falcon Graphic Art Ltd
Wallington, Surrey
Printed in Great Britain by Butler & Tanner Ltd
Frome, Somerset

How To Be A Genius is the distillation of more than twenty years' experience gained by the authors at the Genius Foundation in Leicester. It is aimed both at beginners and seasoned travellers who may have lost their way and stumbled into mediocrity. With handy tips from the world's top artists,* we show that you don't have to be white, male or even dead to be a genius. Now you too can make extra money as a famous artist, writer or composer, get to the top of smart guest lists, be profiled in the colour supplements and have your work on the National Curriculum. Just follow this fun-to-do step-by-step course and watch the world beat a path to your door.

Some sceptics have doubted whether genius can be taught at all. To them we reply, 'Of course it can!' All it takes is a little willpower; the ability to drag yourself over the coals of torment in order to proclaim the truth of your soul; to submit yourself to the rack of despair in the name of your inner fire; to starve, possibly to die rather than compromise your vision; and of course any one of the major credit cards.

It is essential that the exercises included in the text are studied carefully. A regular time of about half an hour should be set aside for practice each day. Make sure the practice room is warm, wear loose clothing and always, always limber up first. A genius accident can lead to permanent incapacitation of your very soul, in which eventuality you'd have to give up the genius business altogether and become an architect instead.

Good luck, and may your labours at the obdurate pit-face of posterity be crowned with magnificence!

Sincerely,
The Authors

---

* *How To Be A Genius* is concerned *exclusively* with geniusdom in the arts – literature, music and the visual arts. While it is possible to become a genius in other fields – science, economics, politics, and so on – these should not be attempted by beginners. You can't just *be* a genius at microsurgery. Believe us. We've tried and the police come.

Contents

1 *The psychology of genius*

> The reason why a work of genius is not easily admired from the start is that there is usually somebody in a big hat standing in front of it.
>
> *Marcel Proust*

> Put that bloody light out.
>
> *Marcel Proust's mother*

Think of genius, and you conjure up images of Mozart writing his first symphony on a Tiny Tears, or of Leonardo, equally at home in a smart smock or functional lab coat. We think of Van Gogh blowing himself to perdition in a cornfield, of Dali dining on his own excrement, of Pound pronouncing himself the midwife of Modernism. Geniuses are prodigies, anguished outsiders, mad eccentrics, raging egomaniacs, and not at all the sort of people you'd want sitting next to you on a coach tour of the Cotswolds.

Here at the Genius Foundation aspiring geniuses ask us the same questions time after time. Are geniuses born or made? Is genius a form of dementia or the ultimate sanity? Does it affect your tax code or life insurance premiums? And, above all, how can we get some of it? So, before we hit the highway to immortality, let us wander through the back streets of history, pause at the traffic jam of dead theories, and join the five-mile tailback that leads to tomorrow.

Divine inspiration
The word genius comes from the Latin meaning 'tutelary spirit of person or place'. In classical times, artistic genius was managed by the nine Muses, goddess

11

daughters of Zeus and Vesta the Swan, who visited the individual in his/her sleep, suggested the outline for tragedy, lyre solo, bust or vase, and took the usual 10 per cent of the gross worldwide. Later the Christian God took over the Arts portfolio and put geniuses under a contract to produce masterpieces anonymously, with a fixed number of Madonna and Child frescoes specified per year. Some time in the mid nineteenth century God died. After this geniuses had to declare their own divinity, often in crowded restaurants.

Detail from
Mantegna's
*Secrets of
Ventriloquism
Revealed*,
1427–9
(private
collection)

Meteoric **Maupassant** on the edge of madness

Neurasthenia

In the nineteenth century, Moreau and Lombrosso argued that genius was a form of neurosis inherited from wayward parents, or acquired via a permissive lifestyle. This appealed enormously to individuals who spent all day in bed whining and all night drunk. Many decadent ne'er-do-wells went round proudly proclaiming they were neurasthenic until the entire hypothesis was discredited. They subsequently switched to Symbolism or became office cleaners.

Zany dramatist **Antonin Artaud** (*left*)
and sculptor **Alberto Giacometti** dry
out at the Acapulco Occupational
Therapy Centre

Physiology

It was briefly believed that Henry James' massive sentences were the result of his huge head. The discovery that Turgenev's brain weighed a staggering two kilos was cited as proof of the theory even though he went a bit funny after they'd replaced it. The notion that size was everything was not fully undermined until Big Bird from *Sesame Street*'s major retrospective at the Museum of Modern Art, after which such reductionist nonsense passed into history and research moved on to more promising terrain such as genetics, cortical function and multi-vitamin tablets.

Gene genie

Although science has located the baldness gene, the snooker gene, and the gene that makes you stick your spoon upside down on your tongue and say 'Yum!' at the end of a tasty yoghurt, as yet it has not succeeded in isolating the gene responsible for hyper-normal creative flair. It has, however, found the one responsible for hyper-normal creative gloom, evidence of which exists in 38 per cent of artists compared to 1 per cent of the general population. At best the resulting chronic mood disorder can produce works of searing insight and exquisite melancholia. At worst it leads to Country and Western music.

Left hemisphere/Right hemisphere

Why are so many artists left-handed, but no good in goal? Can creativity be enhanced by tinkering with the cortex? If you then went on to win the Turner Prize, could you subsequently be disqualified for cheating? The ethical jury is still out on this one.

Psychoanalysis

Freud saw the creative process as being closely linked to early toilet training, mother fixation, the death wish, sublimated ID, the desire to return to the womb and so on, but these days nobody's very interested.

Dynamics of creation

Many authorities have maintained that the reason there are so many more male geniuses than female is that women can fulfil their creative potential and craving for immortality by having babies. Others have pointed out that, while men can't actually have babies, they could at least help out with the night feeds from time to time, and hey! d'you think nappies change themselves? The debate continues.

The young **Will Self** tries music therapy
for his pointed head

Marxist-Leninism

The concept of the genius is a bourgeois scam perpetrated by the ruling class to mythologise élitism. There are only cultural workers, and they'll be visiting the factory today, in the canteen at lunchtime, to perform a short piece and then answer any questions you may have about their work. Please don't throw chairs at them like last time.

Exercises

Easy one to start with. Just fill in the following questionnaire. It's the one we've used for twenty years or more at the Genius Foundation to establish an applicant's IGP (Initial Genius Potential) as well as other aspects of their suitability for the course, such as susceptibility to suggestion and cash flow.

Here again are the main points of the Muse

The IGP Eight-Question Checklist

1 At what age did you complete your potty training?
   a) Less than one year
   b) Less than two years
   c) Tuesday

2 'My heart leaps up when I behold / A rainbow in the sky.' If this happened to you would you ...
   a) Switch to Flora?
   b) Announce it in a poem at the risk of people smirking behind your back in public places?
   c) Hang your head and whimper?

3 Are your hobbies and pastimes ...
   a) Mostly indoors, e.g. chess, stamp collecting, wainscoting?
   b) Mostly outdoors, e.g. walking, riding, shouting?
   c) Mostly shameful, e.g. involving wire wool and membership of the Conservative Party?

4 Do you believe ...
   a) In yourself?
   b) In a deity?
   c) That the John Lewis Partners are never knowingly undersold?

5 Is your self-discipline ...
   a) Honed to a steak-knife edge on the playing fields of Eton or the snows of Kilimanjaro?
   b) Drug dependent?
   c) Mostly shameful, e.g. involving wire wool and membership of the Conservative Party?

6 Have you ever had a personal difficulty you'd rather not talk about?
   a) Mnnn, maybe ...
   b) Uh-huh ...
   c) Hgmnhgnhgmhgnhm ...

7 Is your childlike innocence ...
   a) Buried beyond recall beneath the chaos of acrid adult experience?
   b) Drug dependent?
   c) Pooh-pooh caka?

8 Which credit/charge cards do you currently hold?
   a) Visa/Mastercard
   b) Gold Amex
   c) Get Out Of Jail Free

Sappho updates her Filofax

2 Return to gender

It is only the women whose eyes have been washed clear with tears who get the broad vision that makes them little sisters to the world. When the big sisters come along, kiss your arse goodbye.

'Innovations Catalogue Yearly Digest', August 1773

Since our species first mastered the knack of walking upright, we have denied ourselves 50 per cent of our potential for progress, civilisation, fun, and site-specific installations.

In Britain, the Genius Laws of 1068, which forbade women the right to be bright, imaginative, or inventive in public places (or anywhere in Shrewsbury), remained on the statute books until 1975. In many parts of the world, similar laws are still enforced. To give him his due, William I originally introduced the law as a humanitarian act to regulate the time-honoured practice of burning women with interesting or original ideas, in those days referred to by the general term 'witches'.

As well as legal rights, women have also been denied role models, encouragement, paint, time, money, space, self-belief and food. 'This is John. This is Janet,' said the Florentine School Early Reader Book One – a primary influence on Giotto and his sister Pauline. 'See John. John becomes a precursor of modern sensibility providing a predominantly intellectual organisation to his sensations. See Janet. Janet makes meatballs.'

As will be seen from the ensuing chapters, in order to convince the world that you are a genius, it helps if you can include emotional and sexual incontinence, unruly personal habits, whining self-obsession and aimless misogyny on your CV. Apart from the fact that men are biologically more suited to these activities (you will be given a chance to discuss this later), traditionally women geniuses have had no time for such luxuries, being hard pressed to complete their masterpieces in the few minutes available each day between picking the kids up from school and getting a hot-pot in the oven before hubby got back from his domestic abuse classes. Statistics show that 78.4 per cent more women than men still have to choose between the Life and the Work. It is estimated that one baby equals two novels, twins a trilogy of plays at the National, and a second marriage with several

Helen Chadwick adjusts her site-specific installation, *Gasper Hauser*

Alice B. Toklas bakes a cake for Picasso's surprise fortieth birthday party

Desktop cuisine: busy novelist **Iris Murdoch** prepares lunch before heading for the proseface

Class of '34: taking a break from their easels to enjoy a night out in Taos, New Mexico, are painters **Kay Sage**, **Agnes Martin** and **Georgia O'Keeffe** (photo: A. Stieglitz)

kids each from previous liaisons the complete works of Schubert.

Yet, in spite of this, women have forged a place in the genius hagiography, usually by calling themselves George (Eliot, Sand, etc.).

Mary Ann Evans ponders her literary future

Other traditional ways out of the gender impasse were to become lone beacons, like Jane Austen; to become half of a famous duo (with a parity clause written into the contract); or to join a group. The last two were fraught with difficulty. Being, say, Viv of Viv and T. S. Eliot or Frida Kahlo of Frida Kahlo and Diego Rivera doubtless looked great on the headed notepaper, but rarely protected you from being beaten around the head with a typewriter and/or taken away to the Laughing Factory because you sometimes looked at your husband funny and he put it about that you were barmy. Likewise, just because you were one of the Pre-Raphaelites it didn't stop you from getting the boring jobs, such as filling the opium pipes or lying face up in the water. 'A partnership of equals', was Sartre and de Beauvoir's proud claim, but theirs was an unusual relationship born of existentialism and the fact that they could afford to eat out a lot.

But surely, I hear you ask, things are different these days, aren't they? Ours is an equal opportunities era in which women are given a fair crack of the whip and are free to live the life of Bridget Riley: just as cash machines are completely error-free and Ozzy Osbourne is the head of British Intelligence. But, hell, who said this was going to be easy?

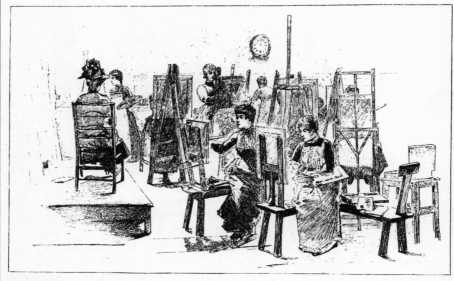

Women geniuses at work

Exercises

For women: Arms outstretched at the sides. Now revolve at the hips reciting as you do so, 'I must, I must, I must unleash disgust.'

For men: Feel like shit.

Sebastian Sprott and **Vanessa Bell**
enjoy a moment of calm by the pond at
Charleston House, Sussex, before
being gatecrashed by a coachload of
Vorticists

3 Home and away

There was a young poet of Dover
Who traipsed and travelled all about
By ship and by train,
By car and by aircraft,
And he still never learned how to rhyme.

Trad.

Now that you have a rough idea of the sort of psycho/social/sexual attributes and equipment you'll need to become a genius, the next thing you'll be thinking about is where to work. Country or town? Home or abroad? Tahiti or Bradford?

Travelling light

The artistic mind has always been attracted to the unknown trail, the voyage of self-discovery. Literature abounds with epic tales of travel – the *Odyssey*, the *Aeneid*, *Heart of Darkness*, *Biggles Flies South*. Many an aesthete of the long haul has been emphatic that it was better to travel uncomfortably than to arrive in a funny mood. What was their motivation, their driving spirit? Here are some you can choose from:

Disillusion Why else would Rimbaud have quit Paris with the world at his feet, not to mention Verlaine's bullet in his leg, and headed off for the South China Seas, Arabia and Abyssinia, never to write another line except to his mother?

Poetic experience Certain locations recharge your batteries and inspire your soul. For Durrell it was Greece, where the only clock is the sea; for Artaud, Mexico with its high mountains, peyote, and street theatre. Wordsworth traipsed the fells. Ingres tried a two-centre holiday combining the Serengheti National Park and the Seychelles. Full details in our Fact Sheet.

The Grand Tour For the European genius, this traditionally meant France, Switzerland and Italy. You started off in funds in Paris, headed across Lake Geneva, then did Florence, Rome and Padua, before running out of money and being forced to hitch back with the Prussian Army and/or pick grapes in the south of France. As travel became easier, the idea of 'doing' the whole of

Car crazy **Francis Picabia** visits **Man Ray** and **Lee Miller** at their country retreat

Eric Gill demonstrates his handbrake
turn to a group of admiring typographers

The **Eliots** set off for East Coker

Thomas Mann visits Venice

Europe in one shot gave way to selecting specific destinations for specific stimuli. You chose Provence for the light and Urbino for the Renaissance hills, Tangier for the oranges, Lake Geneva for getting gothick, Rome for the *dolce vita*, Stockholm for the Ryvita, Sissinghurst for the Harold and Vita, Borussia Moenchengladbach for the UEFA Cup, and Capstan for the fuller flavour. For American Beats, the grand tour consisted of criss-crossing America in a beaten up Chevvy, chewing bennies, constantly risking absurdity and death, balancing on eyebeams on a high wire of your own making, and wearing check shirts. If this appeals, start modestly in pale gingham and get a grown-up to help you saw the eyebeams.

But, some students ask, what if you are a workaholic who never takes holidays, let alone Odysseys? What if you're not a landscape sculptor anxious to cover the Andes in dental floss? Isn't the journey to the East a bit passé? Isn't all travel cultural imperialism? For you, there is the second option of seeing one place through a hundred pairs of eyes rather than a hundred places through one pair of eyes. Novelty spectacles will help with this one.

Centres of Excellence

There are, and have always been, certain places more conducive to geniusing around than others – places where geniuses could meet fellow geniuses and exchange ideas and/or sexual partners. The basic requirements were a Latin quarter, a relaxed attitude on the part of the authorities to outbursts of melancholy, and a good supply of bars and cafés – the traditional meeting places of writers, artists and musicians ever since Aeschylus first ran into Sophocles in an Athenian taverna and, over a couple of glasses of Domestica, invented drama. Given these basic requirements, the rest was a matter of personal taste.

'Think I'll invent an art of psychic tension,' wrote Edvard Munch in his diary as he sat in a smoky Paris nightclub in 1889. 'Maybe I'll call it the Freeze of Life to symbolise those dark, long winters of my Nordic youth.' Like many an artist before and after him, Munch found Paris just about right weather-wise. Not too hot and not too cold. Ideal for writing novels and painting canvases in the open air (see *From Isobars to Wine Bars – Climate and Artistic Migration 1266–1930*, Bill Giles, Airfare Press).

More importantly, Paris was a melting pot of creative fervour. So many disciplines in one place – Cubism, Serialism, Botulism, Narcissism, Innumeracy, to name but four – plus a famous exile round every corner: the Irish escaping religious censorship, the Americans escaping Prohibition, the Welsh escaping.

'Paris is a moveable feast – it is the mobile chip shop of European culture,' wrote Hemingway after a particularly wonderful dinner with the Fitzgeralds at Maxim's. To which Orwell famously replied, 'It's all right for some,' before getting back to scouring the burnt *potage* cauldron at the Café Dent de Sagesse Encastrée.

Ah, those Paris nights! What could be better after a hard day's lonely furrowing than to visit the Lapin Agile, the Deux Magots or the Trois Stooges? Then, at closing time, it was back to Gertrude Stein's place on the Avenue des Lynam in the IVe arrondissement to be ennuied by Braque, étonned by Cocteau and auto-écoled by Peugeot. Every night was Battle of the Bands night, with intense competition between, on the one hand, the Bande à Picasso (Pablo Picasso, lead guitar, Guillaume Apollinaire, bass, Max Jacob, drums) with their criss-cross rhythms exploding into happiness, and, on the other hand, Les Six (Poulenc, Honegger, Milhaud, Beaky, Mick and Titch), who would spin elegiac dissonances into a gossamer fabric of shimmering mystery all kicked into shape by a bad back-beat and a bass in your face. At around four in the morning Sartre and Simone de Beauvoir would turn up, 'Hi, guys and gals,' they'd say. 'Don't you sometimes feel trapped by the nausea of existence?' The party spirit thus destroyed, everybody would suddenly realise they'd left some suicidal despair in the oven, and wander home.

In sixteenth-century London, a good night at the Mermaid Tavern on Cheapside would find the likes of Shakespeare and his sister, Philip Marlowe, Desmond Dekker, Ben Webster, Groucho Marx and Edmund Spenser, Jonson and Jonson, the Earl of Essex and his lovely wife David, Sir Walter Raleigh (the seminal cyclist), and the mysterious Mr W. H. Smith planning innumerable tragedies and generally bitching over a few tankards of sack washed down with a sack or two of tankard. The wit flowed as freely as the drink: 'Put away that dagger, Kit,' they would say, 'before you have somebody's eye out.'

Zurich, in the Dada days of the Great War, was a hotbed of creativity in all areas of accomplishment and activity.

> dans l'église, après la messe le
>   pécheur dit à la comtesse: Adieu
>   Mathilde
> Find was er nötig
> I'll give it five
> Gilly Gilly Ossenfeffer Katzenellen
>   Bogen By The Sea

recited Richard Huelsenbeck, Marcel Janco and Tristan Tzara at the Dada-crazy Café Voltaire at No.1 Spiegelgasse, Zurich in 1916. Just over the road, at No.12 Spiegelgasse, Lenin was sharing a flat with Zinoviev and Radek. A couple of streets away, James Joyce's company of Irish players was performing Joyce's Ibsenesque *Exiles*. Einstein had not long left Zurich for a better job in Berlin, but had just published his General Theory of Relativity and may well have been visiting his old city on a book-signing tour. Over at the barber shop a Mr Lemon Jefferson, yet to be blinded, was inventing the blues. Next door, in the shoe shop, white folks, with ears pressed to the party wall, were stealing it. In a tiny workshop on Gloriastrasse, S. Duncan Black and Alonso G. Decker were revolutionising home sanding. Every Tuesday afternoon, Freud would drive over from Vienna in his van to cure neuroses door-to-door at ten Swiss francs a go. In his new factory in the Industriequartier, Marconi fiddled endlessly with his aerial to try and get a clear signal from Radio Luxembourg. On the Sportplatz, émigré Australians practised long hours to perfect their new bodyline bowling. At the atonal glee club (where Cliff Adams first came up with the idea for Radio 2's evergreen 'Sing Something Complex') Schoenberg's mum kept everyone happy with an ample supply of bratwurst sandwiches. In adjacent laboratories at the Theoretical Pen Faculty of the Universität, Laszlo Biro and Baron Bic worked in furious competition, racing to be first to complete their researches and publish their findings. It all seemed a long way from the trenches. '420,000 British lives lost at the Somme!' screamed the headlines. 'This could

mean war,' commented Lenin, never as politically astute as he was later made out to be.

They were good times, all right.

For some, however, the café society and *vie de bohème* of the European culture centres were not enough. For them the very survival of their tortured vision depended on turning their backs on so-called civilisation and banishing themselves to far-flung shores, where the light was clear, the subject matter elemental, drink was ever so cheap and girls had bare tops.

A few wanted to take it still further and set up a full blown artists' colony where hearts, hands and minds could work in perfect unison and there'd be a Come All Ye every Saturday night. To this end Van Gogh and Gauguin travelled to Arles. Alas, no one else did. Subsequently Gauguin went to Tahiti and Van Gogh to pieces. D. H. Lawrence, too, dreamed up a Utopian community, to be called Ranamin, consisting of a group of like-minded souls led by himself. Disappointed by the take-up, he travelled to Taos, New Mexico, to become Writer-in-Residence in a colony Mabel Dodge Luhan had prepared earlier. Inspired by this model, Kafka applied for the post of Writer-in-Residence at a colony of ants. Predictably, the ants turned down his application on the grounds that he was too creepy by half.

For others the artists' colony was too much of a commitment. The weekend colony was a much better option. To that end William and Dorothy Wordsworth acquired Dove Cottage at Grasmere in the Lake District, and Barbara Hepworth a small tea-room in St Ives. People could drop in when in the area. Though delight-

The **Lakeland Poets** AGM, 1824
(sketch: J. M. W. Turner)

fully informal, the system was inevitably abused by hangers-on, leading to the introduction of a dress code (no beret, no party), membership cards and bouncers.

Today few artists' colonies survive, but that's no reason why you shouldn't start your own. If you have a few bob, and you're not dogged by negative equity, get together with some kindred spirits and buy a run-down barn in the Dordogne. A few home improvements and in six months or so – hey presto! it's waterproof. You can all move in, start painting acrylic fauve landscapes, write about butterflies and, in the evenings, sit around the scrubbed pine Ikea farmhouse table groaning with vats of *daube*, runny cheese and fresh peaches, singing old Elvis Costello songs into the early hours.

Or maybe because you're a Londoner, you love London Town. Bethnal Green is the area to aim for if you're a site-

'Let's do the show right here!' Composer
Benjamin Britten (*left*) hits it off with
vocalist **Peter Pears** at Aldeburgh

specific sculptor. Dalston for painters. For composers, Rotherhithe is the Tin Pan Alley of the avant-garde and the demographic spread of wordsmiths, from starving poets to sitcom hacks, roughly corresponds to an estate agent's price-range map covering Crouch End to Belsize Park.

If you live in Britain outside the metropolis, you'll find that artists' colonies have been more or less completely institutionalised as 'arts centres', so it makes sense to hang around one of these. The typical arts centre was founded on a wave of postwar euphoria and a rationed shoe-string in a deconsecrated chapel renamed 'Phoenix '55'. By 1956 the name was already dated, and its angry young founders, rendered terminally pusillanimous by poverty, turned it into a hula-hoop studio. In the sixties, however, a new group of young men and women with working-class accents, Bolex cameras and coloured shirts took over and renamed it The Arts Laboratory. They instituted a rigid routine of anarchic, experimental psychedelia fuelled by optimism, full employment and the contents of Magic Frank's suitcase. Mondays were happening nights when they would set fire to a piano. Tuesdays were theatre nights when the Rainbow Tangerine People Experience would strip down to their dirty toenails as a protest against Burton's, confront the audience with their, or somebody else's, sexual repressions, and set fire to a piano. Wednesdays were film nights when an enraptured audience would continue to watch the works of Andy Warhol long after the projector had broken down. Thursdays were poetry nights when Roger McGough would set fire to a piano. And Friday night was music night when Electric Groin would play the only track from their latest double album, 'A Very Long Hammond Organ Solo With A Certain

Adrian Henri hits Liverpool 8

Amount of Light Moaning into an Echoplex', and let the piano set fire to them.

The Maoist seventies saw another change. The place was taken over in a bloodless coup staged by 'cultural workers' engaged in challenging dominant modes of production and consumption through integrated practice where feedback discussion was part of the text while wearing boilersuits. Pretence was archived. The name was once again changed to 'The Gas Ferry Project' commemorating the history of class struggle and the right of all workers to become artists. Community Artists went out among the people, encouraging them to confront their oppression by holding self-criticism sessions in bouncy castles. Others, under the slogan 'Children Are Workers Too', formed street theatre companies named 'Captain Magic's Exploding Trouser Circus' who spurred young minds to explore the iniquities of capitalism by wearing saucepans on their heads and shouting to the accompaniment of twelve-string guitars, corroded saxophones and arrhythmic dustbins.

In the eighties the grey people took the place over. The centre was rechristened 'Artspex' and became dedicated not to art, but to arts management, arts management training, arts management training management, arts management training management conferences, seminars, and franchised catering.

But now it's the nineties. The wheel has come full circle. Maybe the great days of café society, colonies, communities and arts centres have passed, but that's no reason why an aspiring genius like yourself shouldn't get things going again. Try the café society thing now. Go on. Go into McDonald's and engage the habitués in a discussion about the bankruptcy of Post-Modernism. Off you go.

Back already? Oh, well. Try again tomorrow.

Exercises

a In 'A Supermarket in California' American poet Allen Ginsberg recalled a spiritual encounter with his spiritual father Walt 'Slim' Whitman in the frozen meat section. John Betjeman, in 'Sanderson Country' describes a similar experience with Longfellow in a wallpaper showroom in Forest Hill.

Next time you're at the shops, see how many famous poets you can spot.

b Drink a health to the wonders of the Western world, the pirates, preachers, poteen-makers, with the jobbing jockeys. (Use a dirty glass.)

GENIUS FOUNDATION TOURS
Booking Conditions and General Information

1. BOOKING

All bookings are made through Genius Foundation Tours which is a trading name of Quinquireme of Nineveh Travel (Kidderminster) Ltd. Once you have decided to bid farewell to England, for it, which has been your cradle, shall never be your dungeon or your grave, a deposit of £65 must be paid for each person including each child, love-child, child of the imagination, child of nature, voodoo chil', father of the man, tabula rasa etc. on making your booking.

2. ALTERATIONS TO TERMS

In all cases Gertrude Stein's dictum – a season in yellow sold extra strings makes lying places – will be taken as legally binding. Thus while we will endeavour to provide in every way your opportunity to build a small cabin in Innisfree (Get-Away-From-It-All Deep Heart's Core Break) of clay and wattles made, with nine bean-rows and a hive for the honey-bee, we can offer no guarantees of your living alone in the bee-loud glade, especially in high season.

Similarly those taking self-catering apartments at Xanadu must be warned that the sea is sunless, and the woman wailing for her demon lover, the ancestral voices prophesying war and the damsel with a dulcimer can at times render normal conversation impossible. Albatross shooting is now forbidden on the Great White South adventure holiday.

3. INSURANCE

Just when we are safest, there's a sunset-touch, a fancy from a flower-bell, some one's death, a chorus-ending from Eurpides. We have, therefore, negotiated good value premiums for top grade insurance which gives above average benefits for baggage, delayed departure, sunset touches, flower-bell fancies and Greek tragedies.

4. PACKING HINTS

Kerouac travelled with nothing but his own confusion; Cliff Richard with only a pocketful of dreams and a heart full of love, and they weigh nothing at all. Joyce observed that the Roman, like the Englishman, brought to every new shore on which he set foot only his cloacal obsession. William Carlos Williams vouchsafed that liquor and love rescue the cloudy sense, banish its despair and give it a home. You decide.

5. HEALTH

- You must take off your clothes for the doctor, and stand as straight as a pin, his hands of stone on your white breast bone, where the bullets all go in.
- Do not take a bath in Jordan, Gordon.
- Make sure you know the difference between waving and drowning.
- Watch out for fever at Missolonghi and don't go sailing in the bay of Spezia.

6. GENERAL

Beware of expecting too much from your holiday. Pleasure is very seldom found where it is sought; our brightest blazes of gladness are commonly kindled by unexpected sparks.

4 *Having talent*

Talent is a myth invented by dullards who use their lack of it as an excuse for being too idle to get off their arses and become geniuses.

Exercises

Cover your left nostril with the thumb of your left hand. Now hum down the nose and, using the little finger of your right hand, pluck 'Pop Goes The Weasel' on your right nostril. Aren't you talented!

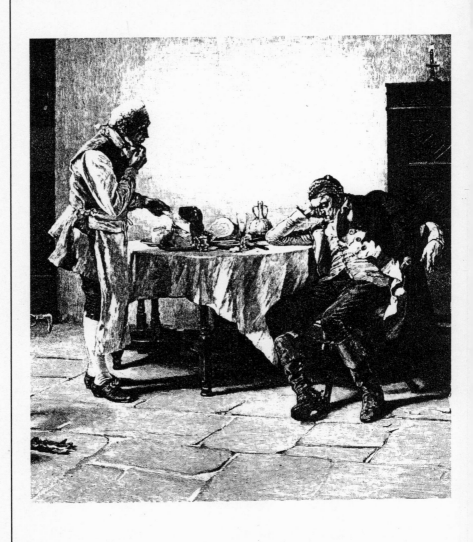

Maxim Gorky gets his idea for *The Lower Depths*

5 *Inspiration I: Get anguished – be happy!*

One joy scatters a thousand griefs. Then what?

Ha Suong, 'The Song of The Human Juke-Box'

'Where do you get your ideas from?' is the question most often asked of geniuses.

Nietzsche describes how the plot and themes of what was to become *Also sprach Zarathustra* seemed to invade his mind while he was out walking above the Bay of Genoa. At other times, in the same place, he became convinced that Pontius Pilate was saying rude things about his neckwear. Likewise Mozart intuited whole scores while travelling in a carriage outside Vienna. 'Where the ideas come from I know not. Nor can I force them,' he subsequently recounted to his hypnotist.

The wonderful thing about waiting for inspiration is the way it leaves you free to tile the bathroom, go to the pictures or cook for friends. Be warned, though: interrupted inspiration can prove devastating. We all know of Coleridge's Man from Porlock. Less well known are Britten's burst water pipes during the cold winter of 1947. The cautious genius never underestimates the importance of lagging.

Popular composer Sir Peter Maxwell Davies dreams up his zany brand of modern music while water-skiing around his beloved island of Hoy, near Scotland. 'I

FOR SLALOM SKIING PLACE SECOND TOE BINDING UP CLOSE TO HEEL

HEEL

TOE

4½"

FIN

9" BEFORE BENDING

12"

3"

3½"

3½"

MEASURE OUT FROM CENTER LINE OF SKI TO PLOT CURVES

FRONT

25½"

BACK

FRONT
19 'KERFS CUT
IN TOP SIDE OF

got the idea from Claude Debussy, who sadly died seventy-six years ago,' explains Max. 'He composed his three symphonic sketches, *La Mer*, during the 1905 Surfing Championships at Eastbourne, where he came third.' Sir Peter can often be seen zooming around the Orkneys in search of inspiration, with fellow composer Harrison Birtwistle at the helm of their powerful speedboat, 'Deathtrap'.

'Occasionally, if it's a nice day, we may ski over to Fair Isle to check out the latest pullover patterns, which I sometimes use as the basis for musical notation,' says Max.

Statistically, suffering, mental or physical, has been the most common source of artistic inspiration down the ages. 'All I do is cast my rod in the sewer of despair and see what comes out,' Francis Bacon used to advise his fishing pals. Geniuses are rarely strangers to suffering. Milton was blind, Beethoven deaf, Delius had syphilis, Keats consumption. Byron had a funny foot, Van Gogh was mad, Strindberg thought he was an elm tree, Sibelius had sensitive teeth, and most of the others spent their lives in sexual, bisexual, multi-sexual, mega-sexual or 'anxious about shoes' torment of one sort or another.

But how much suffering do you need for how much art? Could you write, say, a small piano sonata on no more than

Van Gogh: sold only one painting in his lifetime

Seasonal Affective Disorder? If you went out and got your toes crushed by a fire engine, what would be your chances for a Booker Prize?

A common error is to confuse art *about* suffering with the suffering artist. Art is not just a convulsive expression of personality. It exists at a crucial distance from its creator. Chekhov, Kafka and Beckett all explored themes of alienation, loneliness, pointlessness, but in private were fun-loving guys. Beckett even wore a revolving bow-tie and played pinchy-winchy with dead people. Similarly the Expressionists held up a cracked and peeling mirror to a cracked and peeling world but then went out for a burger, took in a show, and partied till dawn.

Beethoven, being deaf, lonely, ugly and horrible, had plenty to get upset about, but he didn't go on about it. On the contrary, he wrote, 'Artists are made of fire – they do not weep.' He died shaking his fist at the overhead thunder and never attended a men's group in his life.

RUMBLE...

DONNER UND BLITZEN, I NEED A SHOT OF RHYTHM AND BLUES!

Picasso believed that suffering was not so much a source of inspiration as a means of advertising your genius: thus, for him, actual suffering was less important than convincing others of his suffering. Often referred to as 'the genius's genius', Picasso pulled off this stunt in spades. An early success and a rich man most of his life, he commuted in fancy chauffeur-driven cars between his various studios in the nobby districts of Paris and his various chateaux on the Côte d'Azure; a virtual stranger to the anguish of love, when one of his wives or mistresses left him he invariably had a couple of substi-

Nice 20/viii/44

tutes waiting on the sidelines; apart from constant hypochondria and a late spot of prostate trouble, he enjoyed rude good health and, in spite of smoking two or three packs a day, lived till he was ninety-one. And yet, somehow, he always managed to project an image of torment and despair – a man at odds with his own soul, haunted by the spectre of death. The main means by which he achieved this sleight of hand was simply telling people. 'I am tormented,' he would say, stuffing his face with fancy cakes at the Tour d'Argent.

'Look at me! I am in despair,' he would shout, walking down the Champs-Elysées with banknotes falling out of every pocket and a ballet dancer on each arm. 'I am at odds with my own soul,' he would howl from behind the smoked-glass windows of his Cadillac. 'I am tortured by the constant presence of death,' he would weep, aged eighty, while doing press-ups on the beach with an untipped Gauloise stuck out of the side of his mouth, having just sired another couple of children.

Philosopher **Friedrich Nietzsche** (*left*) and poet **Walt Whitman** backstage at the Grand Ol' Opry

Nordic misery **Edvard Munch** knocks
up a while-u-wait portrait whilst waiting
for his suit to come back from the dry
cleaners'

Coco Chanel and **Pablo Picasso**: just good friends

Nevertheless, a random glance through recent history reveals a lot of individuals who never mastered this trick and were forced, by the dictates of their chosen career, to spend all day and night up to their necks in disconsolate mire. The beginner would therefore be well-advised to devote at least a portion of each day to concentrated anguish, if only to be on the safe side.

So what's the best kind of anguish to start on? Bitterness resulting from an unhappy childhood? Poverty? Sickness? Rejection in love? Self-hatred? The Death of God? – always a blow, especially if you were looking forward to a church wedding.

There can be no hard and fast rules, but, again to be on the safe side, it's best to go for as many as possible all at once.

So, let's get anguished! The exercises below are probably the most important in the book. You will never regret time spent mastering them for they could provide you with a lifetime of satisfying and productive misery.

Reluctant genius **Richard Wagner** visits a health spa in search of a cure

Exercises

a Check out your family tree. Were you born (i) astride the grave; (ii) in a cross-fire hurricane; (iii) in a trunk? Did you find your teddy floating upside down in a stream? Does your chewing gum lose its flavour on the bedpost overnight? Did you chew plaster/walls as a child. If not, give it a shot now.

b Freewheel from skid row to bedlam. And back. And rest.

c Either (i) construct a palace out of your own excretions, or (ii) become a graveyard chewed over by the worms of remorse. Make sure you tidy up before lunch.

d In rhythm with your own heartbeat have an intimation of immortality closely followed by a *nostalgie de la boue*.

e Squat position. Twenty 'Auld Lang Synes'. (Not to be attempted south of the border.)

f Begin by despising yourself, riches and others. Gradually build up to dying in a pool of your own vomit/blood. And rest.

Barrel of laughs: the irrepressible **Mark Rothko**

Jean Baptiste Corot: always painted to
the music of Roy Orbison

6 Inspiration II: Sex, drugs and bacon rolls

Niaga dessip tsuj I ma ro tnorf ot kcab gnitirw siht si?

from the notebooks of Leonardo da Vinci

Robert Graves said, 'To be a poet is a condition rather than a profession.' Many large towns have at least one pub where, towards closing time, non-professional poets in a poetic condition lament the world's lack of understanding of their gifts before going home to mark Year 9's geography tests.

Most works of art are alcohol-related offences. The usual line is that pain resulting from the unique insight and imagination granted to the gifted and great can be dulled only through tragic and self-destructive dependency on alcohol and other drugs. In fact there is very little evidence to suggest that this pain-desensitising thing works. Artists are still miserable buggers even when pissed.

But historical precedent tells us that you have little chance of becoming a genius unless your life is given to dissipation and debauchery – or if not a whole life, at least a 'wild period' lasting from a few weeks to several years and possibly repeated from time to time in order to prove

Vintage verse: poet and homebrew expert **Stephen Spender** treading grapes at his chateau near Nuneaton

something or other, like you're still pretty good at losing your overcoat, falling over, hitting your head on sharp things, and going 'wagga wagga' at shop windows. It may mean wrecking lives and hotel rooms.

You may shock yourself. You may shock your family and friends. You could end up a fluttery-eyed dipso with a hole in your wallet nearly as big as the one in your heart and nothing to show for it but blank eyes and a sense of waste. This is definitely the nasty side of being a genius, but it's got to be done. Just keep telling yourself 'the road to excess leads to the palace of wisdom', don't forget to drink a pint of water before going to bed and have a bucket handy just in case.

Here's some dos and don'ts about hellraising:

DO keep things properly organised. If you're about to embark on a Dionysian quest, but are not sure whether to begin with a pint of Newcastle Brown and a couple of Neurofens or the full lost weekend in the opium den, why not make a neat wallchart, listing all possible vices, and tick them off as you go along? That way you can decide which activities provide the most inspirational stimulus. Know your poison. Drink or Drugs? There is a fine tradition of alcoholic geniuses which you might like to become a part of.

Proust: duvet flashes

Brahms and Liszt, for instance. But **DO** remember that alcohol damages the liver and necessitates frequent trips to the toilet – a particular problem if you're a Northern Novelist of the 1950s with only shared outside facilities. For this reason you may prefer to go for substance abuse. Coleridge, Byron and Shelley were all slaves to laudanum; Aldous Huxley experimented with mescalin; William Burroughs injected himself with live lobsters; his brother, Edgar Rice, used to go 'Yeoeoeoeoeoeoeoeoeghghghgh' in public.

DON'T feel it is absolutely necessary to ravage your body to get high. The health-conscious modern genius may prefer to take smart drugs round at the brain gym.

DO experiment with new sources of the creative high. 'My heart aches, and a drowsy numbness pains my sense as though of hemlock I had drunk,' said Keats. Some people get the same thing with a couple of Victory Vs. You should be so lucky.

DO decide whether you want to be a solo lush, a husband and wife duo, or part of a hellraising bratpack. (NB Solitary drinking, though cheaper, can result in maudlin self-pity and is best not attempted without an emotional safety-net tested to BS 19473826.)

DON'T drive. Ever. Geniuses do not sit behind the wheels of Vauxhall Astras. They just don't. They walk. They take cabs. They ride in droshkys. The only time it was ever OK to drive was in the late fifties/early sixties when it was permissible to drive coast to coast across North America stopping only for gas and dex. Now, even that's thought silly.

Stormy Monday: Olympic-class drinker **Malcolm Lowry** drives a lawn-mower to the bar after a lost weekend left him carless

DO pace yourself. A short, tragic life looks good on your posthumous CV, but can be fatal, and is not to be recommended if you plan a late flowering. So, if you don't want to end up on a filthy mattress existing on sardines out of a tin and craving a drink, take a tip from the bohemian's bohemian, Rimbaud, who blazed into Paris in 1871 on a sea of absinthe, opium and scandal, wrote some of the best poetry of the century and then quit before he got burned out. Here at the Genius Foundation, most of our second- and third-year students have already decided that it's better to be a living legend than the corpse of a nonentity. The rest are dead. Luckily we take a full year's subscription in advance.

Does hellraising enhance creativity?

Run a few simple tests. Go on a bender but carry on working. Does the work stand up? Can you stand up? Invite an art critic, literary agent or Radio 3 producer round for a second opinion. Alternatively go out and buy a Self-Delusion Meter from Do-It-All, take some opium and monitor the ensuing insights.

On balance, the advice has to be this: don't do drugs, kids. Is a short-term high really worth having to spend the rest of your life being venerated by rich, glamorous people in London, New York, Paris and Rome?

Sex

Throughout history male geniuses were supposed to have bigger sex drives than the voyeur on the Clapham omnibus. The Great He assumed exclusive rights to the Muse, and, on announcement of his genius, expected blow-jobs on demand from women who were led to believe that refusal would be a betrayal of a sacred trust bestowed on them, as women, by future civilisation. Their role was to inspire, encourage, flatter, please, satisfy and make the sandwiches.

Male geniuses are no longer granted special licence to abuse their fellow creatures. These days Byron, rather than having a rakish reputation for being 'bad and dangerous to know', would be dismissed as a sexually and emotionally dysfunctional date-rapist.

The alternative to all this misogyny and nastiness – highly recommended for

> ORGASM IS PURE THOUGHTLESSNESS, YEAH?

> IT CERTAINLY IS IN YOUR CASE, ANDRE.

beginner, intermediate and advanced geniuses alike – is to be gay. Ancient Greek geniuses had to be by law. All Renaissance Italians were by choice. So was every French poet except two. Everybody who went near Bloomsbury was – even those just riding past on a 24 bus. Indeed, the more you think about it, the more you find yourself drifting towards the inexorable conclusion that *all* geniuses were gay, but a lot of them were scared to own up in case they were sent to prison like Oscar or their mums found out. Forceful arguments in favour of this theory have been put forward by many experts in the field, notably Sir Edward Grassmeyer in the trenchant and insight-

ful paper published in *Horse and Hound* (7th March 1958), entitled 'Landseer Was All Right, But Let's Face It All The Rest Of Them Were Bloody Nancy Boys'. Since Grassmeyer's day the theory has been further researched and its most recent proponent, Charles Knudsen, summarised the evidence in a brilliant lecture series delivered in my back garden while he was clearing the gutters at the top of the kitchen window, pointing out that:

1. W. H. Auden never spent much of his time doing up classic cars.
2. You never saw Benjamin Britten down the football.
3. David Hockney is not what you'd call a married man.
4. Virginia Woolf could whistle with her fingers.
5. Stands to reason, doesn't it?

O mes amants, [wrote Paul Verlaine]
Simples natures
Mais quels tempéraments!
Consolez-moi de ces mésaventures.
Reposez-moi de ces littératures;
Toi, gosse pantinois, branlons-nous
  en argot,
Vous, gas des champs, patoisez-moi
  l'écot,
Des pines au cul et les plumes qu'on
  taille,
Livrons-nous dans les bois touffus
La grande bataille
Des baisers confus.

If you like a bit of fun, get hold of a French dictionary and a hanky. You're in for a treat.

Exercises

a Turn off your mind, relax and float downstream. (Thirty repetitions, fifteen left, fifteen right.)

b Write a poem on an olive. Put the olive into a very dry Martini. Drink the Martini. Drink several more Martinis. Breathe your breath against the sky. Take the piece of sky between your fingers. Put it in an envelope. Send it to Yoko Ono. She likes that sort of thing.

Popular Russian tunesmith **Nikolai Rimsky-Korsakov** gets the idea for his overture *Scheherazade* in a St Petersburg takeaway

7 *Inspiration III: Seize the moment*

Art cannot exist in a vacuum. It clogs up the filter
and you find yourself having to change the bag more
frequently than should be necessary.

Peggy Guggenheim

Essentially, all art is, in a sense, so to speak, the very expression, as it were, of its cultural moment – the *Zeitgeist*. Or is it? For sure, Late Romanticism, the apotheosis of dominant male culture with its strivings, yearnings, apocalyptic climaxes and orgasmic resolutions, undoubtedly reflected nineteenth-century

End of an era: ploughmen discuss nemesis in the work of Thomas Hardy, c. 1890

imperialism and technological rape of (Mother) Nature. Expressionist art happened in a milieu of early twentieth-century social upheaval – new technologies, psychoanalysis, political unrest, religious uncertainty and unreliable motors. Cubism, Serialism and Einstein's Theory of Relativity undoubtedly share a common basis – they make your head hurt.

The hardest and to some extent the most crucial craft the aspiring genius has to master is how to encapsulate the spirit of our own age; to seize the moment; to be the voice of a generation; to surf the *Zeitgeist*.

Luckily all this can now be done by machine (pictured right).

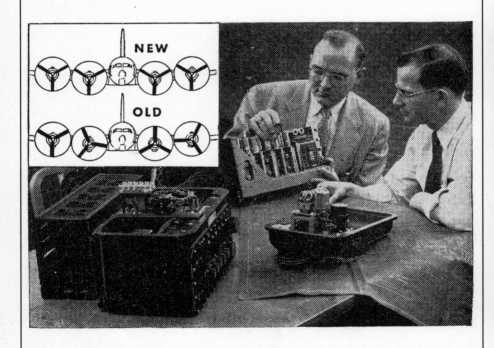

Art and Science: **Erasmus of Rotterdam** explains to **Leonardo da Vinci** how to get out of the Middle Ages

Exercises

Seize the moment. Put it in your pocket. Save it for a rainy day.

Florentine School convention, c. 1540

8 *Business aims I: The Manifesto*

There is no question and no answer. There is an announcement.

Bob Holness, 'Blockbusters Redefined'

By now you should have your environment sorted out, your inspiration flowing, and you're probably pretty keen to get going on that tone poem, verse tragedy or mixed-media assemblage. But wait a mo! Are you sure you know what you're doing? Put down your brush, your pen or your oboe and let's have a long, hard think about our *aims*. What are you hoping to achieve? What is art for? How does it relate to society, philosophy, politics, metaphysics, historicity, ontology, entelechy, thatness, hypostasis, aseity, and all those other words on page one of *Roget's Thesaurus*?

Throughout history it has been the artist's compulsion not only to paint, draw, sculpt, write and compose but also to talk bollocks – what Hemingway called *cojones* – about why they're doing it. Indeed, in tough artistic circles, if you can't talk the *cojones*, you're politely asked to leave the café table and make room for a real genius who can.

Art is a business. No business can do business without very clear aims. Good businesses make it their business to describe these aims in a document, defining clear goals and a code of practice, often with a catchy title such as, 'Guttering Into The Future', or 'Soap Dispensers and Disposable Hand Towels 2000'.

In the genius world, this Business Aims document is known as the Manifesto, best written as part of a group. Check to see whether any groups operate in your area (look in *Yellow Pages* under 'Avant-Garde'). If there aren't any, you could start your own by placing an ad. on the local arts centre noticeboard, buying some draft manifesto forms from W. H. Smith and laying on some cheese and wine. When choosing a group, make sure it has *...ist* at the end of the name. This ensures that its ideas form a proper *...ism*, and they're not just a bunch of cowboys. Besides an *...ism* always looks good on your CV. See the end of this chapter for a list of suitable *...isms*.

OK. Let's write a manifesto. The key

words here are bold, stirring, and stupid.

I smash drawers ...

said Tristan Tzara in his manifesto of 1917. Not perhaps the most revolutionary of declarations but certainly worrying for anyone who likes to keep his socks nice.

... those of the brain and those of social organisation ...

This is more disturbing, everybody likes to keep their brain drawers nice.

Everywhere to demoralise, to hurl the hand from heaven to hell, the eyes from hell to heaven, to set up once more, in the real powers and in the imagination of every individual, the fecund wheel of the world circus. Order = disorder; self = not-self; affirmation = negation; ultimate emanations of absolute art.

This is manifesto writing at its very best – a precise statement of beliefs and business aims finishing with an excellent catch-line for the letter heading – 'Ultimate Emanations of Absolute Art. VAT Reg. 294 584 01932'. The only quibble one could make is with the document's failure to include ballpark figures or to set specific targets. Something along the lines of

to hurl the hand from heaven to hell *within the next six months*, the eyes from hell to heaven *in two years max.* and to set up the fecund wheel of the world circus *by 1922 at the latest, all within the budgetary restrictions outlined in the F&GP Committee's document of 11th inst. weighted for inflation*

would be better.

Checking their manifesto for printing errors are, from left to right, Surrealists **Paul Eluard**, **André Breton**, **Anatole France**, **Louis Aragon** and **Man Ray**

The Dadaists were great manifesto writers, as were the Surrealists. The Futurists wrote nothing else. Of equal value for the student, however, are some of the lesser-known manifestos.

Death! Murder! Lust! Blood! Revenge! Incest!

runs the first line of the Manifesto of the Minor Jacobean Playwrights, although after that it tends to lose its way a bit, and it's incredibly long.

We declare these truths to be self-evident, that all men are created equal, that they are endowed by their Creator with certain unalienable Rights, that among these are Life, Liberty, and the Pursuit of Happiness

ran the first lines of the Plagiarists' Manifesto of 1777, before segueing inexplicably into the Ninth Book of *Paradise Lost*.

We find ourselves supervising the nativity of a purifying revolution, upturning the social, political, religious, moral, intellectual and artistic institutions, beliefs and standards of our age,

ran the Bloomsbury Group's first newsletter.

Our aim is to construct something new; we are in the van of the voices heralding a new society which should be unfettered, rational, civilised, and dedicated to truth and beauty. Eventually we hope to be able to afford a new minibus and go on tour.

Manifestoism leads inevitably to schism, as when, in the late nineteenth century, a small but aggressive faction of Sunday Painters expressed a wish to do a bit of sketching on Bank Holiday Mondays and precipitated a row which led, ultimately, to the Franco-Prussian War.

The inaugural meeting of the
Brotherhood of English Ruralists

You may not, on the other hand, wish to join a formal group. If you're a bit shy you may wish to remain a lone maverick like Ibsen, or abhor meetings like Palestrina. Don't feel you have a duty to join in. Duty is, to some, the negation of creativity. Better, perhaps, to be duty-free and join a less formal grouping, like the Pointillists. They met just twice a year and then only to discuss the minutes of the previous meeting and decide whose turn it was to offer a Join-the-Dots puzzle for the Xmas raffle.

Exercises

a If order = disorder; self = not-self; and affirmation = negation, complete the following:
    i) truth = ?
    ii) trousers = ? (careful)
    iii) a bird in the hand = ?

b Make a wallchart of the following. Do not take a moment's rest until you have learned it by heart.

ISMS AND GROUPS AT A GLANCE

Pointillism nineteenth-century painting movement which produced light effects by crowding the surface with small spots of colour

No-Pointillism forerunner of Existentialism

Abysm an archaic form of *abyss*. A big hole

Modernism another big hole (B. Sewell)

Romanticism nineteenth-century movement much taken with turbulent emotions, grand gestures and swirly scarves

Imagism movement of poets opposed to Romanticism. Advocated precise imagery, clarity of form and leopard-skin pill box hats

Imaginism revolutionary Russian movement proclaiming no possessions, no heaven or hell, and all the people living in the world go 'oh-ho'

Pseudopseudohypoparathyroidism the third longest word in the *Oxford English Dictionary*

Surrealism twentieth-century movement whose members advocated the bypassing of intellect and the primacy of the dream, to be achieved by bizarre happenings, automatic writing and zany visiting cards

Spoonerism admiration of pine faintings

Expressionism proclaimed the primacy of inner experience to be expressed by making films called *The Cabinet of Dr Caligari*

Abstract Expressionism 1940s/50s American movement whose adherents painted with one hand, drank with the other, and sometimes incorporated their own vomit into finished works

Nepotism twentieth-century movement believing that everyone working for the BBC should be called Magnusson

Galvanism movement founded in nineteenth-century Birmingham, dedicated to stopping their buckets rusting

Geophagism eating dirt

Cubism eating lumps of sugar

Cubophagism eating Cubists

Neocubolesbophagism eating Picasso's portrait of Gertrude Stein

Futurism violent departure from traditional forms of art, music and literature, starring Michael J. Fox

Alcoholism catch-all term often used as a synonym for 'art'

Onanism another common synonym for 'art'

Chism film starring John Wayne

The Decadents nineteenth-century group whose members renounced the natural in favour of the artificial and sat in darkened rooms discussing Satanism and listening to Black Sabbath albums backwards

Dirty Realists group of American writers who patented the fishing and fucking novel

Impressionists late twentieth-century movement pioneered by Mike Yarwood and brought to its zenith by Rory Bremner

Tokenists group of casting directors who often gave women or Asians the role of 'Second Doctor'

Mindbenders followers of Wayne Fontana, sometimes called 'The Modern Masters'

The **Pre-Raphaelites** waiting for
inspiration

Marlowe – genius or life insurance
salesman?

9 Business aims II: Shocking the bourgeoisie

Boo!

Charles Baudelaire

In the previous chapter we described something of the style and layout you should adopt for your manifesto, but what should it actually say? What after all *is* the aim of art?

One could, of course, spend several years discussing this. Many people have devoted a whole lifetime to the subject, and when you're a genius you'll have the leisure, and indeed the obligation, to do so too. What the aspiring genius needs, however, is a fast and easy answer to get going. On the whole there's only one aim of art really worth pursuing at least in the early stages – it's a good one, and some have stretched it out for their whole career – and that's the aim summed up by Baudelaire in his injunction: 'Il faut épater le bourgeois.'

'Il faut épater le bourgeois.' Learn it. Properly, in French. Repeat it nine times every morning when you get up. Translate it into your own words and work it into your manifestos. Sew it in your scarf. Tattoo it on a family pet. Eat it for break-fast. Have sex with it. Swap train numbers with it. Above all, say it to your friends. See how impressed they are? Shocked even. Sometimes so shocked they drift over to the other side of the pub and pretend they're very busy reading beer-mats.

Actually Baudelaire only meant one bourgeois, M. Bougon, his nextdoor neighbour. It's a long story, the gist of which is that Baudelaire had this neighbour called M. Bougon who used to complain about Baudelaire putting his dustbins out the night before the bin-men came, rather than the morning they were due. M. Bougon said that this attracted rabid dogs and unwholesome cats to the area. Also M. Bougon wasn't keen on Baudelaire's Satanism, particularly when he forgot to draw the curtains. 'You don't want Beelzebub's dripping maw gawping at you out of a front bay every time you pop out to the off-licence,' he used to say. 'It puts you off your Mackeson.' Understandably, Baudelaire found M. Bougon's constant complaints intensely irritating, so he became a genius as a way of getting back at him. It worked, too. In later years when critics, pundits and noblemen mentioned the poet's name in hushed, reverent tones, M. Bougon always felt guilty and shabby and small-minded. 'If I'd known he was going to be a famous poet, I'd never have mentioned the bins,' he used to say. But it was too late. Anyway, when Baudelaire first said 'Il faut épater le bourgeois,' he only meant M. Bougon, but, over the years, it's come to mean the bourgeoisie in general.

'Il faut épater le bourgeois.' It's a real corker of an aim isn't it?

'Il faut épater le bourgeois.' The only problem with this one comes when some prodnose who knows nothing about geniuses asks. 'Pourquoi?'

This is a tricky one, so pay attention.

Originally artists were not allowed to be bourgeois. They were of the artisan class. Painters worked in workshops, not unlike a modern garage. There would have been a shop at the front with a few off-the-peg works on sale, and a studio at the back. Each place was run by a master, Giotto, say, or Raphael, who would have a team of assistants and apprentices sweeping up, grinding the colours, filling in bits of the sky and so on. Customers would come in and say, 'How's the *David Espying Bathsheba* coming along?' and Giotto would wipe his hands on an oily rag, suck his teeth, and make no promises, but he could have it ready by Thursday depending on whether he could get the parts from Luton.

Composers were employees either of a church, a city or a rich man. All day long they'd diddle diddle dum. They would be expected to run a couple of choirs, an or-chestra, compose and play special pieces for dances, weddings, funerals and bar mitzvahs, write operas if there was a theatre, teach the kids and generally make themselves useful about the house. Play-wrights and actors, even if they had their own theatre and patron, were still socially at about the same level as the man who sucks a mouth organ outside the reces-sion shop these days. Poetry was a side-line and there were no novels.

Ladies and gentlemen were allowed, indeed expected, to play a bit of lute, draw a view, and write sonnets, but only in an amateur capacity, much as it's now acceptable for a merchant banker to put up the odd shelf.

Then this is what happened.

In 1504, Michelangelo and Leonardo were hard at work in the Council Cham-ber at the Palazzo Vecchio in Florence: Michelangelo on his *Battle of Cascina*; Leonardo on his *Battle of Anghiari*. Chat-ting, they began to grumble about the rate of pay for the job. This led to a more gen-eralised lament about the status of the artist in society.

In order to remedy this iniquity the two painters resolved to put aside a little money each week with which to bribe writers to puff them up. It worked. Castiglione, in exchange for a bagful of ducats and a helicopter, wrote his *Book of the Courtier*, which suggested that paint-ing pictures and so on were inherently more dignified trades than, for instance, gutting swans. Vasari, after receiving most of the profits from the *Crucifixion of St Peter* and a lovely set of chisels, wrote *The Lives of The Artists*, idolising Michelangelo in particular. So well did Vasari do his work, that the painter him-self began to believe his purchased plau-

Follow that! Husband and wife fiddlers **Nicolo** and **Doreen Paganini** upstage the opposition with a novelty finale to their stage act

dits. In the later years of his life he often sat on the heads of people who refused to call him 'The Divine Michelangelo' and blew bottom wind into their faces, even if they were Popes.

By the eighteenth century, all artists were believed to be touched by this divinity. Hogarth's Copyright Act gave a legal status to the product of that divinity, by defining the conception of the work as a property distinct from the canvas and paint, and made it easier for artists to get mortgages. Furthermore the rise of the middle classes had broadened the market for art. Artists grew wealthy and their social status rose. They liked this. They bought detached houses with conservatories, shopped at Debenham's, went to dinner-dances. In keeping with their new status, they gave up their old workshops with their artisan connotations, and worked alone, adding more weight to the image of the individual possessed of a divine inner vision.

The social status of musicians, and even writers, rose in a similar trajectory. But let's stick with painters for a while.

With so many respectable middle-class painters, every one of them supposedly touched with divinity, selling so many pictures to largely undiscriminating middle-class buyers who just wanted a few nice portraits for the wedding album, or a view of the house to give to the estate agent, the problem then arose: how was the outstanding artist supposed to distinguish himself from his run-of-the-mill co-workers? Two methods suggested themselves.

The first was to take a leaf out of the Romantic poets' book and be mad, bad and dangerous to know – all the usual genius

Sharing a joke at the Abstract Expressionists Dinner-Dance are **Jackson Pollock** (*left*), **Lee Krasner** and **Mr** and **Mrs Franz Kline**

stuff contained in this book: drink, debauch, deflower, die and so on. This got your name in the papers, did nothing to harm your divinity – gods, being above the morals and mores of society, do that sort of thing all the time – and gave the buyers of your work a vicarious frisson of danger themselves.

The second method, and this was more risky, was to produce works which nobody would possibly want to buy. This severed the final link with the old artisan tradition and convinced the world that your driving force was definitely no mere marketplace, but the divinity itself, the tortured 'I', the inner truth, heard by no other. It was a daring stunt, but if you could pull it off the rewards in fame and money were tip-top.

Now, although it may seem like it to the casual reader, this wasn't some elaborate con-trick perpetrated by a conspiracy of artists, critics and intellectuals to defraud a semi-gullible public. Since divinity, inner truth and value, like beauty itself, are all in the eye of the beholder, if enough people believe a thing to be divine, true, valuable and beautiful, then so it becomes. That's the way it is with reality. It's fluid. Even scientists don't believe in reality any more, and they're real people. So loosen up. Hey look, here comes a parallel universe. Whoops, there goes another rubber-tree plant. 'The Emperor's New Clothes' is a story for the naively mean-spirited who, knowing nothing of the psycho-bio-socio-philoso-Harpo-linguaphone-theological ways of the world, are convinced the world is out to get them and smug when they think they can tell. Art, like an interesting haircut, is alien to such people, and all three should bewilder them.

Fig.1 Reality fluid

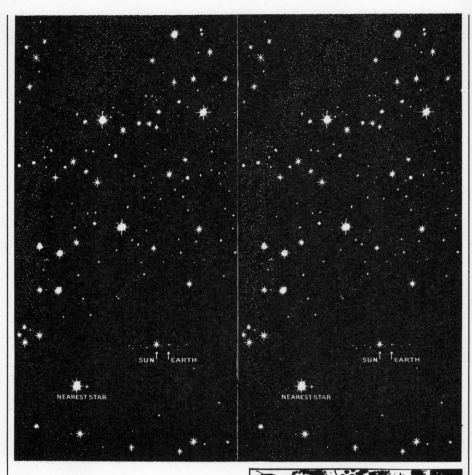

Fig.2 Parallel universe

Fig.3 Rubber-tree plant

At every level, for the genius, shocking the bourgeoisie isn't an activity so much as a process of self-verification. If the bourgeoisie don't understand what you're doing, it's working. If you don't understand what you're doing either, even better – the difference being that you couldn't give a monkey's. And you know the right clubs to go to.

Some people will tell you that there are no bourgeoisie left to shock. Others will say that the only people who can't identify the bourgeoisie are the bourgeoisie themselves. Ha! And to you, Notary Public Beneficio, I say, 'Put down your ink-pots and your sealing wax and come join in the dance of Cultural Uncertainty!' And to you, Alexandr Alexandreyevich Protopopov, I say, 'Play me the Song of Universal Disorder you used to play when we were children, before the soldiers came, and I will beat time on my loud drum and then, perhaps, we will forget our hunger.' And to you, little Anya, I say, 'Let the dreams of youth never be dreams of despair. When you find yourself walking naked through the shopping mall of destiny, except all the shops are selling little kittens and snakes, and there's a big red train coming out of the tunnel to run you over, fear not the Freudian implications. Flaunt your stuff!'

A more serious problem is that most of the really shocking feats have already

The **Berlin Dadaists** elect a chair for their first meeting in 1915

been used, and anyway shock-value is an ephemeral quality. All Baudelaire had to do was go up behind M. Bougon, say 'Boo!' in a loud voice, and M. Bougon was well and truly *épaté*-ed. That's how easy it was for the Symbolists.

Others had to try harder. De Nerval walked a live lobster through the streets of nineteenth-century Paris on a piece of

Fig.4 Lobster

string; the Dadaists stood on stage and shouted, 'Honour can be bought and sold like the arse. The arse, the arse, represents life like potato chips; and all you who are serious-minded will smell worse than cow's shit'; Francis Bacon shouted, 'I want to be fucked by Colonel Gaddafi', in crowded DIY stores; Gregory Corso suggested throwing the coffin across the room at Kerouac's funeral because it 'was the kinda Zen thing Jack woulda dug'. In the old days, when confronted by this kind of thing, the bourgeois often fell over they were so *épaté*-ed. But the bourgeoisie are a resilient lot. You throw a urinal in their face one day; the next they bid millions for it at Sotheby's. The angry jet of bile turns into a period text. Is it still possible for the artist to wrench preconceptions from the sticky flypapers of complacency and cause the whole sorry edifice of polite society to collapse under the weight of its own hypocritical contradictions? Or is the best result you can expect a bit of mouth-foaming from Brian Sewell? Where should the student genius begin?

Rapturous reception: **Laurence Olivier**, seen here in an offbeat production of *Coriolanus* with **Joan Plowright** as the lucky gal

Face up to the difficulties and have a crack at it. Don't worry – you needn't necessarily take all your clothes off. Reject the past, recreate the present, forge a new tomorrow. Spraycan 'CENTRAL LONDON HELIPORT' on the steps of the Tate Gallery. (Practise with a bit of waste hardboard at home first.) (Oh, and make sure you get permission.) Use a Henry Moore bronze as a novelty ashtray and then say you don't smoke. Take your bowling balls to a Chopin recital at the Purcell Room and afterwards try to claim it was a genuine mistake. Steal a pizza delivery bike and ride through the Cottesloe Theatre shouting 'I'VE GOT THE MOST LIVER OF ANYBODY HERE!' Project thin films on to next door's washing line. Perform street theatre on a Scalextric track. Hold a major exhibition in Chris Serle's breast pocket without telling him first. Or abandon art altogether and become an encyclopaedia salesman. Honestly, the commission's smashing.

Different: *éminence grise* and Steptoe-lookalike **Bill Burroughs** once wrote a novel in a Mexican urinal

Wacky artist **Marcel Duchamp** shows TV host **Johnnie Carson** some of his ready-mades

Exercises

Take a small bourgeois (you can buy practice bourgeois from most branches of Top Man). *Épate* him. When you've *épaté*-ed one side, turn him over and *épate* the other. (About 20 mins.) (Do not, at this stage, attempt to *épate* both sides at once.)

10 *Getting down to it*

Genius is an infinite capacity for taking pains.
True genius is the ability to do it another way.

'The Sunny Smiles Book of Deep Thoughts'

At last, let's get going!

Art, whatever else you may say about it, is a job. Not a proper job, like working for Kwik-Fit Euro, admittedly, but still you have to get up at some time of day or night and put in a few hours' labour at the canvas, the piano or the typewriter in order to earn the crust.

Let us first address ourselves to the problem of where to work. At home or in a Pizza Hut? In a brightly lit studio or a rat-infested hovel? Proust worked in a cork-lined room, Wordsworth in a state of emotion recollected in tranquillity. Although it is fairly easy to construct a serviceable opium haze, the working environment favoured by De Quincey, many local authorities get sticky about the planning permission.

Some experts put great emphasis on the need for solitude. Henry James advised young writers that 'the word you must inscribe on your banner is loneliness'. Wagner on the other hand couldn't write a note without an entire orchestra in his garret, with anything up to twelve cymbals players. Mrs Gaskell worked with her studio door open to the street so that passers-by could point in and remark, 'See her? Mother of Provincial Realism.' Try them all to see which suits you best – let your imagination run riot. Remember, in the bedroom nothing should be considered 'dirty' or 'too way out'. As long as you and your partner are in agreement

Ravel: built his own shed

Dr Johnson: got his from a garden centre

and both enjoying yourselves, anything goes! Sorry, we just seem to have drifted into the mysterious world of Dr Alex Comfort.

Clothing is very much a matter of personal taste, bearing in mind that no genius ever turned up for work in a double-breasted suit or tasselled loafers.

Hardy always wore his lucky trousers to write the Wessex Novels. Robert Tressell wore ragged ones for his major opus. Bach worked in loose-fitting Dr Scholl's to tap out the organ riff. Brecht favoured a black polo neck until mid-life dandruff made it inadvisable. When choosing your wardrobe, take note of function. For a messy abstract, gardening trousers should suffice. For an angry young diatribe, how about something shamefully outmoded from Mr Byrite?

When choosing your tools, unnecessary expenditure on fol-de-rols such as a curly palette or a top-of-the-range Apple Mac is a sure sign of the amateur and will cause stifled laughter. If Woolworth's rulers were good enough for Mondrian, they're good enough for you.

Tools of the Trade: in an era of sophisticated word processors, Post-Modern writer **Martin Amis** prefers to pound out his purple prose on a battered Remington

Perspiration

It was Thomas Edison who coined the maxim: 'Genius is 1 per cent inspiration and 99 per cent perspiration.' It has only recently been realised that deodorant too has played a small but vital role in the history of art (see the very seminal, not to say pungent, *From Musk Ox to Fruit Salad*, Anita Roddick, Airfare Press, £39.99). The ability of the early *plein airistes* to endure the hot Barbizon sun for hours on end was only made possible by the invention of Mum Rolette at the then embryonic Laboratoire Garnier; and you didn't stand a chance of getting a one-person show at the Robert Fraser Gallery in those crucial years between 1965 and 1969 unless you had that pop-icon the Sure Extra-Dry tick somewhere about your person. Many now believe that D. H. Lawrence's refusal to use deodorant – he went to bed in the same vest for six years in order to retain the earthy stench of his Midlands roots – is the only interesting thing about him.

Pictured receiving his Working-Class Novelist of the Year Award is **Mr D. H. Lawrence** of Nottingham

An urban sculptor orders some derelict wasteland from the council and plans how many old washing-machines, cars and fridges he will need for his show

The block

Now it comes. The blank page. The silent piano. The empty canvas. The anxiety of making that first mark. All represent the limbo of terror through which the spirit of true genius must pass on its way to immortality. On a tour of the Alps with her husband Percy and Lord Byron in 1816, Mary Shelley describes a severe attack of writer's block:

> I thought and pondered – vainly. I felt that blank incapability of invention which is the greatest misery of authorship, when dull Nothing replies to our anxious invocations. 'Have you thought of a story?' I was asked each morning and each morning I was forced to reply with a negative.

Don't worry, this kind of mental constipation is common. It's caused by thinking too much and can be relieved by a dose of mental Syrup of Figs, e.g. a Meatloaf album with the bass turned up. In Mary Shelley's case, the laxative was Lord Byron's legendary skiing accident when, with typical bravado, the 'Hucknall Eagle' attempted an off-piste, on-piss slalom, finishing with a breathtaking 104-metre V-style jump which went horribly wrong and landed him in intensive care. Seeing him the next day, stitched up, strapped in plaster, clamped in all manner of surgical appliances with a bolt through his neck, Ms Shelley went straight back to their chalet, and wrote *The Munsters*.

The annals of Western culture are full of such stories, most of them invented by Sir Kenneth Clark, but some of them are true and they remain a lesson to us all. As Picasso said, 'In not seeking, I find.' Whether you are looking for a rubber band in the kitchen drawer or raking the em-

bers of your consciousness for a spark
to light the Flame of Inspiration, the same
rule applies.

Work avoidance
People often asked Beethoven whether
he spent a set number of hours each day
composing, or did he waste a lot of time
fiddling with his bald patch and reading
Ann and Nick in the then popular day-
time newspapers? Being deaf, of course,
he never heard the question.

Lunch on the job for prolific composer
Ludwig van Beethoven

Théodore Géricault on the set of his
Raft of the Medusa

Research is the most common work avoidance tactic. Braque would search the cafés of Paris for days on end looking for people with rectangular boils and goitres to serve as models for his cubist vision. Rossini, dressed in a black mask, rode hundreds of miles on a white stallion to test the possibilities for long-term popu-

Four-legged research: **Gioacchino Rossini**

Emile Zola helps **Flaubert** find the right word

larity of his *William Tell* Overture. Paul McCartney devoted many years of research into the behavioural characteristics of amphibians before composing 'The Frog Song'.

The business
When they actually get down to business, some geniuses work with painful slowness, others with breathtaking speed. Graham Greene wrote his novels at the rate of one letter a month, and sometimes not even that. Having agonised over the capital 'D' which gives such a forceful opening to *The Honorary Consul*, three months passed before he was able to fol-

low it with a compelling lower case 'q', another three before he realised, having consulted many dictionaries and other reference works, that there aren't any words beginning 'Dq', and yet another six months before he was able to scratch out the 'q' and replace it; first trying a deflationary 'f', then a sublime 'v', and finally, perhaps feeling that what he had lost on the roundabouts of style, he had gained on the swings of literacy, the 'o' on which he eventually, after many sleepless, tortured nights, settled.

Picasso, on the other hand, is estimated to have produced some 50,000 works in his lifetime. Admittedly he started young

Turning his hand to a short story at Arnold Bennett's Black Country Realism Workshop is **Somerset Maugham**, watched by daughter **Susan** and the managing director of Tie Rack

and worked until he dropped at the age of ninety-one, but, say he got properly going at fifteen, that still comes out at nearly two works a day, 365 days a year. A lot of people can't paint that fast even with a roller. And art was only his secondary interest, the primary one being shagging.

Similarly Edgar Wallace usually dictated a full length novel before breakfast, another during breakfast, another on the lavatory after breakfast, and, by the time lunch was brought in, had seventeen or eighteen new works, proof-corrected, printed, bound and arranged in alphabetical order in his personal library which was converted from a disused airship hangar.

Trollope wrote at the rate of one thousand words an hour so exactly that for a while they used him, his desk perched high on a pedestal in Paddington, to time the comings and goings of the Great Western Railway.

Coleridge often wrote poems in his sleep. Andrew Lloyd Webber has written musicals in somebody else's sleep; and had them performed while the audience was in a similar state.

Robert Louis Stevenson managed three thousand words a day, most of them 'Yo' or 'Ho'. Henry James was even more productive, often completing between sunrise and sunset the four or five thousand words he needed to make a complete sentence.

Modigliani, depressed by failure to sell his work, declared: 'I do at least three pictures a day in my head. What's the use of spoiling canvas when nobody will buy?' His untimely death, at the age of thirty-five, from what the coroner diagnosed as 'linseed oil poisoning and the pressure of excessive impasto on the inner surface of the occipital region of the skull', should serve as a warning to all who would follow his example.

Exercises

Think of one hundred ways of avoiding getting down to it using only a writer's block. (Chisels may be used.)

Weirdo composer **Anton Webern** gets to grips with serialism

Thomas Carlyle's disapproving wife
Jane lights the fire with the manuscript
of his racy novel, ***** Me Backwards*,
now lost

11   *Genius management*

The farmer with his girlfriend lay,
Down in the long grass making hay,
Eee, by gum, the things they say,
When I'm painting haystacks.

Claude Monet, 1891

Claude Monet, Impressionist painter and banjulele virtuoso, wrote many such ditties which went down a storm at the Giverny Women's Institute, but at the time were thought to have no lasting merit (see *Artists of the Barbes Longues School*, David Cottington, Airfare Press, 1990, £39.95). Monet's long-overlooked lyrical ephemera are now seen as unique documents – day-to-day observations as important as Corot's sketchbooks, Delacroix's journals or Van Gogh's letters to his brother, Roosevelt Sykes. In fact, Monet's songs are currently being reissued on a CD compilation by Waldemar Januszczak, using period instruments.

Managing your genius means not throwing **anything** away: notes, sketches, scribbled jottings on napkins or menus, interdepartmental memos, ansaphone messages, holiday snaps, dry cleaning tickets and VAT receipts. Keep copies of letters you write, also the replies (unless they're more witty/profound than yours).

Such curatorial diligence in the archive department pays off. Priceless letters changing hands at recent London auctions included correspondence between Publius Ovid and Jesus Christ, Karlheinz Stockhausen and Lord Montgomery of Alamein, Jacob Epstein and Lenny the Lion, Gustav Holst and the young Norman Vaughan. If no one else writes to you, sit right down and write yourself a letter and make-believe it came from someone else. Write yourself offers of professorships, proposals of marriage and general fan mail. File everything – correspondence, press clippings, nail clippings – for as sure as God made little green apples, some day, somewhere, some twenty-first-century PhD student will want to exhume the scattered shards of your life's work and reassemble them into the lamp of destiny from which, with a few brisk rubs, your genius will re-emerge, brightening the sky like a new star and lighting the way towards a new tomorrow.

Sadly many artists have faded into

A recently unearthed photograph of **Arnold Schoenberg** (*on drums*) with members of the Second Viennese School

oblivion simply because they lacked an organised filing system. Don't let this mistake be yours. Secondhand two-drawer filing cabinets are available from the Genius Foundation for as little as £95. Ones with handles for £130.

Other artists have been more fortunate, but more through luck than design. Several major works, long thought lost to posterity, have emerged from beneath crumbling linoleum and the backs of cobwebbed pianos. Samuel Beckett's unproduced, and probably unread scripts for the BBC Radio serial, *The Archers*, commissioned just before his death (published for the first time below); a fragment of one of Edgar Varèse's settings of Verlaine's 'Poetry for Lonnie Donegan'; and the full set of Petrarch and Giotto's 'Stars of the Pre-Renaissance Variety Theatre' collector cards, commissioned by CoCo Popes, His Holiness's Favourite Breakfast.

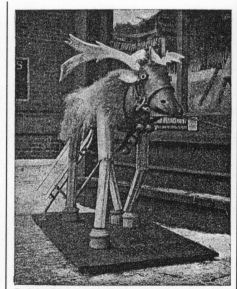

Pablo Picasso's early design for Muffin the Mule

THE ARCHERS

EPISODE 3.983

by SAMUEL BECKETT

GRAMS: Sig. tune.

SCENE 1

A DUNG HEAP.

NELSON GABRIEL AND JOE GRUNDY STAND NEXT TO EACH OTHER. BOTH ARE ENCASED, FROM THEIR FEET TO THEIR NECKS, IN FRESH DUNG.

<u>JOE</u>: Oeeeeoooooeeeuuuuh!

<u>NELSON</u>: For heaven's sake, what is it, Joe?

JOE COUGHS FOR THREE OR FOUR MINUTES.

<u>NELSON</u>: For heaven's sake, what is it? Joe. What is it?

PAUSE.

For heaven's sake.

SILENCE.

<u>JOE</u>: It's. Nothing.

SILENCE.

<u>JOE</u>: Nothing comes, nothing goes, nothing happens. It's an everyday story of country folk. It's awful.

SCENE 2

A FIELD

JACK WOOLLEY AND LINDA SNELL LIE ON THE GROUND IN THE ATTITUDE OF DEATH.

<u>JACK</u>: Oh, Caroline. Oh, Peggy. Oh, Jean-Paul. Oh, my pacemaker. Oh, Captain. Oh, Captain.

<u>LINDA</u>: You should have let me organise things.

<u>JACK</u>: Oh, I realise that, now.

<u>LINDA</u>: If you'd have let me organise things it would have all been better.

<u>JACK</u>: Better?

<u>LINDA</u>: Better.

<u>JACK</u>: Better than what?

<u>LINDA</u>: Better than they were before.

JACK: Oh, before. Some of us can't really remember before. Can you?

LINDA: What?

JACK: Remember.

LINDA: What?

JACK: Before.

LINDA: When?

JACK: The days when things weren't better?

SILENCE.

LINDA: No.

SILENCE.

JACK: Oh, Caroline. Oh, Peggy. Oh, Jean-Paul. Oh, my pacemaker. Oh, Captain. Oh, Captain.

SCENE 3

A DUNG HEAP.

NELSON GABRIEL AND JOE GRUNDY STAND NEXT TO EACH OTHER. BOTH ARE ENCASED, FROM THEIR FEET TO THEIR NECKS IN FRESH DUNG.

JOE: Oeeeeooooooeeeuuuuh!

NELSON: For heaven's sake, what is it, Joe?

JOE COUGHS FOR THREE OR FOUR MINUTES.

NELSON: For heaven's sake, what is it? Joe. What is it?

PAUSE.

For heaven's sake.

SILENCE.

JOE: It's.

SILENCE.

JOE: Nothing.

SILENCE.

JOE: It's.

SILENCE.

JOE: Nothing.

THEY DO NOT MOVE.

NELSON: I can hear a ring.

GRAMS: Sig. tune.

Experts gather to authenticate **El Greco**'s autograph book

Exercises

a In the worst scenario, your bid for posterity could be down to as little as a single line in the *Oxford Dictionary of Quotations*. Devise it now. Something along the lines of 'Only connect', or 'I'd rather be dead than bored'. Try to be simultaneously original, pithy, deep, funny, sage and onion.

b Write out, in your own hand, the complete text of say, William Golding's *Rites of Passage*. Sign it with your own name and date it 1973 – i.e. seven years before the book was first published. Put the manuscript under your floorboards, or somewhere it won't be discovered for a hundred years or so. You never know.

c Do not go gentle into that good night, or at least not without first memorising a list of mediums you might wish to contact after your death.

Gertrude Stein in pensive mood

12 *Enigma variations*

Those for whom the sacred Muse
May immortality ordain
If they're caught wearing slip-on shoes
Are very soon forgot again.

Thomas Gray, 'Elegy in a Branch of Saxone'

We live in a media age. Image is everything. In the past genius could, perhaps, have passed muster on product alone, but even then a smart creator with good management knew that a little enigma wouldn't come amiss.

Looking the part

Baudelaire defined Dandyish Beauty as consisting, above all, of 'an air of coldness which comes from an unshakeable determination not to be moved; a latent fire which hints at itself and which could but chooses not to burst into flame.' The man was cool. Even M. Bougon had to acknowledge that. Not for him the clichéd Raybans or the portraits-next-to-a-wall that had bedevilled press-packs ever since the Baroque.

You want to look modern, but not naff: intelligent, but with a hint of sassy. A visit to one of our style gurus here at the Genius Foundation should clear up most of your problems.

The first thing they'll deal with is the

Yves Tanguy: inventor of hair gel

hair. Beards are still essential for male painters of a certain age. A long white one for the ancient genius, a short goatee for the middle-aged young bohemian. Female poets too should work hard to cultivate a few wisps. The powdered wig may once have been *de rigueur* but the contemporary rug is a sure sign of artistic insecurity. Rather opt for baldness, it never did Picasso any harm, nor Telly Savalas. Anyway, if you're a proper genius you should be wearing a hat. At the turn of the century it was briefly thought that imagination, like heat, could be lost through the skull. Although science has since discredited this theory, geniuses are superstitious folk, so, to be on the safe side, most wear hats in public, in private and in earnest. You'd be a fool not to do the same. By convention,

Joseph Haydn: considered nose job

Artist **Robert Rauschenberg** (*left*) features the traditional goatee whilst contemporary **Jasper Johns** goes for broke with the Engelbert Humperdinck 'tache'

Hat check (*clockwise from left*):
Auguste Rodin sports an elegant
stetson while **Ezra Pound** opts for
desperado chic with a battered fedora;
Leo Tolstoy favours the communard
cap and **Toulouse-Lautrec**'s king-size
bowler doubles as a secret drinks
cabinet

male, and many female, novelists wear a battered trilby until their sales exceed 50,000, when they are allowed to switch to a panama as a badge of their success. Only amateur painters still wear the basque beret: professionals favour a stocking cap. Peaks are also passé.*

But more important than any other aspect of appearance is the *pose*. The genius should pose at all times, until no gesture or movement is ill-considered, but particular attention should be paid to the detail of posing when being photographed for a book jacket, album cover

A professional hat thief about to make off with schizoid composer **Bob Schumann**'s inspirational homburg

*Rather a lot of hats in this chapter. [Ed.]

or exhibition catalogue. Pose, pose, pose and pose again. The photo shoot is one of the artist's best opportunities to say to the world, 'This is me. Fuck you!'

George Eliot was one of the first to exploit its potential, posing moodily for H. P. Robinson outside Coventry Cathedral for the export paperback edition of *Middlemarch*. Nowadays, a few props and the correct angle can produce an entire mystique. Practise at home. Position several mirrors in such a way that you can see yourself as others see you. Try the following poses until you have made each look at least partially convincing. Use Michael Ignatieff as a guide to what is meant by 'partially convincing'.

(a) *The 'lost in my own brilliance' stare*

Hold the index finger flat against the side of the cheek, with the other fingers folded, their knuckles resting against the lower lip. Incline the head down (avoiding sideways tilt) at an angle of 33 degrees. (Get the angle right; any more and it will look as if you should be in intensive care, any less and it will look as if you've had an accident with the Superglue.) Make the eyes vacant. Frown slightly as if trying to pursue a thought too deep for meaning. Or smile grimly as if you've just observed an irony which nobody else could possibly understand.

(b) *The 'I refuse to let you see how sensitive I actually am' semi-crouch*

Sit with your arse on the very edge of a chair, leaning forward with the knees apart. Allow a couple of locks of your hair, if of an appropriate length, to fall forwards. Clench the hands between the knees until the knuckles show white. Tighten the lips. Stay in this position for a long time even though it makes you want to go to the toilet. The effect is also ruined if you fall off the chair.

(c) *The 'Oh my, Oh my, such a world, such a world, so much input, but I'm on top of it' wipe*

Stand. Tilt the head forward. Run the fingers of both hands through the hair from the front to the back (if bald a moment or two's deep massage of the scalp can have the same effect). Take the hands all the way to the back of the neck and then round to the chin. Clench them, with thumbs beneath the chin and fingers above, head still down. Stay in this position for a few seconds, allowing a gleam of excitement to sparkle in your eyes. Then, suddenly, look up and say something – just one or two words, it doesn't matter which – in a foreign language.

Perhaps the easiest and most rewarding way to become an enigma, and to bypass all worries about image, appearance and posing is simply to disappear. Rimbaud quit poetry at nineteen and sodded off out of postcard contact. Rembrandt went AWOL for ten years, leaving his portraits for his apprentices to finish. Nobody has seen Thomas Pynchon for thirty years. Paganini never did interviews. Ditto Salinger and Renoir. Beckett had a phone which didn't take incoming calls. Siegfried Voverney never existed at all. And there's no such thing as a free lunch.

Exercises

   a Grab your coat and grab your hat.
   b Vanish.
   c Hello. Is anybody there? I said, hello, is anybody there?
   d Well done.

The seventeenth-century **Dutch School**
out looking for Rembrandt

Raymond Carver says:

Remember Kids -

DON'T DRINK AND WRITE!

13 *Those whom the gods love ...*

I'd rather be dead than bored.

Goethe

You are.

Monsieur Bougon

Henry Wallis's painting *The Death of Thomas Chatterton* is, for many, the archetypal image of the Tragic Genius: young, romantic, consumptive, abjectly poor and, above all, dead.

The greatest career move any genius can make is to die. One of the most difficult decisions an artist has to take, therefore, is how and when to die. Reputations have been destroyed by an ill-conceived or mistimed death.

The trick is to die as young as possible, leaving a small *œuvre* which, while it may not be so good in itself, demonstrates great potential so that subsequent biographers can bemoan the loss to humanity caused by your demise.

Dylan Thomas (eighteen straight whiskies in a New York bar at thirty-nine), Sergei Esenin (hanged himself at thirty), Vladimir Mayakovsky (shot himself through the heart at thirty-six) have all vied for Chatterton's laurels. Only two have come near: Yukio Mishima (public hara-kiri on a balcony in central Tokyo at forty-five) and Rick Nelson (freebasing while at the controls of his own aeroplane at forty-six).

An attractive alternative is starving in a garret, except, of course, for the starving part. For most people, however, this is no longer an architectural possibility.

You could try starving in your attic, crouched next to the cold water tank, or in the cupboard under the stairs, but somehow these options lack pathos. Starving in a loft conversion will invite the question, 'If he could afford a loft conversion, why was he starving?'

No, best to go for suicide. The manner and timing can be completely controlled, and it also ensures that your last words are, indeed, your last. Death by natural causes can easily catch you in the middle of saying something ungainly or mundane. After a life given to gnomic utterance, 'Can you get me a *Smash Hits* if you're going to the shops, love?' is not a good finish.

As Nijinsky (kidney failure after thirty years of barking insanity) put it, 'I can't dance, don't ask me ... every dance is the dance of death, particularly the hully gully and the watusi. But not death of the body. The body lives, but the soul dies and becomes a dove, in God and of God. I am a dove. I am God.' Later he also became a horse.

Blast from Hell: former Vorticist
Wyndham Lewis at the mighty
Wurlitzer, Theatre de Luxe, Gloucester

Exercises

a Don't even think about doing the exercises for this chapter until you've finished the book and put in an order for some of the exciting products and other courses available from the Genius Foundation.

b And don't forget to read the small print.

Small print
Statistically, the split between artists, poets etc. who were struck down in their prime and those who were struck down in a geriatric ward is about 50-50. This is a gamble you have to take – whether to burn yourself out before thirty in case that's all you get, or to go for the long, index-linked option of pacing yourself. Remember, the level of good ideas may go down as well as up. Who's to say whether Schubert, Shelley or Seurat would have sustained their level of quality output had they lived to pensionable age? Longevity, as Billy Connolly said, is the revenge of genius.

And what about the mature works of Turner, you may ask, if you're still awake – or Beethoven's late quartets? Or Goya's bleak, terrifying visions from La Quinta Del Sordo, subsequently closed down under Health and Safety Regulations? 'Life', wrote the seventy-nine-year-old Verdi at the end of his hit musical, *Falstaff*, 'is but a joke.' On balance it is better to take the chance. Like a great claret, it is certainly possible to become, with age, more profound, more luminous, more lucid, more in the sky with diamonds, more like that bit of the Planets Suite with the celestial chorus fading away into the undulating depths of cosmic oceans, echoing through dark eternity beyond all words, beyond language, their timeless mantra. 'A wop bop a lula a lop bam boom ...

Mrs Gaskell, seen receiving her Mother of Provincial Realism Award, 1849. Mr Gaskell (*front row, sixth from the right*) looks on. Her boyfriend Damien (*back row, standing*) looks browned off. The people in front are nothing to do with the event. They've come for the indoor bowls championships and are in the wrong hall.

14 *Close that sale*

Early to bed, early to rise, get drunk and self-mythologise!

Old genius's proverb

While it is by no means necessary, and rarely even advisable, to sell the fruits of your artistic vision, many aspiring geniuses worry about the day-to-day inconvenience of malnutrition and wonder, if they are destitute, how they are to afford the paintbrushes, drink, drugs, funny hats and so on that are the necessary trappings of genius.

There's no harm in having a day job to keep body and soul together, as many precedents betoken. Chekhov continued to practise as a doctor even after he had found success as a dramatist; T. S. Eliot worked as a banker and publisher until *Cats* went platinum; Strindberg plied the madman's trade.

Ezra Pound once worked as a driving instructor for the BSM. One of his pupils was W. H. Auden. The interesting thing about this fact is that, although it isn't true, its veracity, or lack of veracity, is irrelevant to an understanding of the works of Pound or Auden. This is called Structuralism.

Jacopo Bellini (1400–1470), Gentile Bellini (1429–1507) and Giovanni Bellini (1430–1516), known collectively as the Flying Bellini Brothers (although Jacopo was, in fact, father to the other two), were one of the most popular acts of the Venetian State Circus, charming Renaissance audiences with both their trapeze daring and their mastery of perspective and chiaroscuro. The only painters of the Quattrocento to wear leotards, they specialised, of course, in ceilings and are reported to have been able to complete a creditable *Creation* or even a *Christ Turning The Moneylenders Out Of The Temple*, from start to finish, and execute a series of breathtaking triple reverse somersaults with one-hand passes and no safety-net before the band had got to the third chorus of 'The Sabre Dance'. Sadly, few of their frescoes have survived: the plaster would crack each time the Big Top was packed up and the circus left town. For this reason they became early pioneers of oil-painting, finding it the ideal medium for canvas. Their masterpieces, *Madonna on a Unicycle*, *God Passing the Bun of Life to Jumbo the Elephant* and *Christ Crucified on a Sea-Lion's Nose*, can all be seen at the National Gallery.

Many aspiring geniuses, however, would argue, quite rightly, that there's no point in being a genius if you still have to have a proper job, punch a time-clock, get up in the morning, contribute to the biscuit money, and think of something witty to write on the big card for Christine's leaving.

In the old days the trick was to seek the patronage of some semi-enlightened half-heartedly benevolent Prince, Lord or Cleric. These days patronage is more likely to come in the form of a government grant (often called a Giro) or a

business sponsorship scheme (often called shoplifting).

Without a patron or sponsor, the artist is thrown into the marketplace; to schmooze and network with critics, agents, promoters, publishers, gallery owners, and wealthy buyers. Let's look at the techniques involved.

Patronage

Ludovico Sforza patronised Leonardo da Vinci from 1482 to 1500. Most of the time it was downright humiliating for 'clever little Leo', as the Duke called him, but da Vinci had to endure it stoically. In the fifteenth century there was no shortage of psychopathic princes and mucky Popes willing to hand out a couple of buckets of ducats for a major monument or a son-

Landed gentry: traditional sponsors of the arts

net cycle. The ideal patrons were cultural aficionados of enormous generosity, who would leave their protégés to their own devices and focus on the minutiae of administration – handling the petty cash, ordering the wine, arranging for programmes and invites to be printed, settling the hotel bills and keeping the prurient press at bay. At one time Cosimo de' Medici (1389–1464) had forty painters, thirty-two sculptors, nineteen poets, forty-five castrati, six heretical philosophers and an eleven-piece banjo band on his books.

Those days are gone. In most European countries, the benefactors of old have been replaced by state patronage in the form of grants, commissions and awards. Although Britain is near the bottom of the league table when it comes to supporting the arts, it is still possible to con money out of your local Arts Board if: (a) your idea is wacky enough, (b) it benefits the local community, (c) you know the people on the panel. Arts administrators are a benign enough bunch. Mostly well-meaning liberals, chosen for their ability to discuss ring-fencing, match-funding and to read three-inch thick spiral-bound consultative documents without laughing, they are the liqueur chocolates of the art world – sweet brittle exteriors full of famous names which they drop all over you. So give them a call ... they're in *Yellow Pages* and they'd be glad to hear from you. Simply explain that you're a genius, living locally, and that your work seeks to engage with contemporary social issues within the parameters of your experimental and/or investigative approach to your medium, and to enable you to develop creatively within a cultural context, would they please come across with ten grand of what is, after all, public money which is once again, as is so often the case, in danger of being syphoned off into top-heavy management and extravagant conferences.

They'll probably invite you to meet the advisory panel of your choice, or even to join it. But the Arts Council itself is increasingly prey to market forces, and artists are once again encouraged to tout their wares in what Big Ron called the marketplace, which in some ways is no bad thing, in other ways no good thing, and in *Every Which Way But Loose* Clint Eastwood romped with an orang-utang. Andy Warhol, with characteristic candour, announced that 'the best Art is business Art', recognising that in the age of mechanical reproduction art is a commodity and that genius is measured in royalty cheques. Richard Strauss was one of the first composers to capitalise on this: sheet music sales of his 'Four Late Songs' ('My Love is a Restless Stream', 'Down By The Poplars I Grieve for Thee,' 'Eventide' and 'What Time Do You Call This?') with chord charts for ninety-piece orchestra, grossed over a million. Patrons, collectors, heads of multi-nationals and anybody called Saatchi can usually be persuaded to pay over the odds for the visual arts, being people with what psychologists call 'more money than sense', but sponsorship, too, brings problems. Who can, for instance, forget the recent RSC production of *Macbeth*, which included the lines

> The Thane of Fife had a wife: where is she now? What! will these hands ne'er be clean? Jif Microliquid, where are you?

Daredevil poet **Philip Larkin** raising funds for a new art gallery scheme in Hull

Or the farce at the ENO when the aria, 'Your Tiny Hand is Frozen', from *La Bohème* was interrupted by a chorus of plasticine tortoises extolling the virtues of night-storage heaters.

> ACCORDING TO THIS, THERE SHOULD BE THREE OF YOU.

Bernard Delfont negotiates a London Palladium season with the **Brontë Sisters**

Were things really any different in those ostensibly happier times of readily available patrons? Did the length and tedium of his work on the Sistine Chapel stunt Michelangelo's development as an artist? If he had not been a slave to the demands of his patron, might he not have invented air-brush technique and completed some slick album covers?

The relationship between artist and patron has never been easy. Geoffrey Chaucer, the 'Father of English Poetry', records in his diaries details of several stormy meetings with his patron, John of Gaunt:

14th Aprille 1387: Aprille's a bitche of a monthe. Olde Gaunte, time-hounor'd Lancastre, did sende roond a mesaungere to saie his maister wolde speke with me.

The olde baistard was inne foule tempe. 'Whats thisse I hear aboot the new poeme?' asketh he.

'Its ycleped The Caunterbury Tayles,*' saith I. 'Its aboot a pylgrimauge.'*

'Pylgrimauge schmylgrimauge,' saith he. 'I hyrre you to wryte seculare poemes inne vernacular. If I wanted religose stuff Idde hyrred a byshop, for Crysake.'

'It is seculare, I promyse ye. And its inne vernacular. Gimme a chaunce!' I beged. 'I trow youlle love it when ye rede it. Honnest.'

'I rede sum of it alreddie,' replyde the olde baistard, 'And I telle, what I rede I dont lykke so muche.'

'Whats the praublem, bosse?' I asked.

'Wyrre loukinge at a verray competytyve markette for poetrie out there at his moement in tyme, Geoffrey,' saith he, 'And unlesse youre poeme has that lyttle somthynge that maketh the paunteres sytte up and take notisse, wyrre alle up shytte creke sans paddelle.'

'And by a lyttle somthynge, I trow ye meanne ...'

'Tyttes and asse, Geoffrey. Yme talkinge tyttes and asse.'

'For Crysake, bosse, theyre on a pylgrimauge!'

'Thats my pointe inne firste plaise, Geoffrey. Youre sujecte matters alle wronge. Maybe we could sayve it. Maybe I sholde bringe inne oon of themme Ytalianne guyyes – maybe Dante or Boccaccio – to kicke a little spyce into it. Rawnch it up a lyttle.'

This mayd me sikke to my stomyck. Tray monthes worrk had I putte in on thysse poeme and here was Olde Gaunte tellynge me he wasse goynge to hande it over to the woppe reryte doctors.

'Maybe I colde do the rawnchynge,' I proposed. 'Maybe I colde mayke the knight a lyttle lesse parfit and gentil.'

'What aboutte the pardoner and the summoner? Coldent you makke them a lyttle bitte rawnche too?'

'A rawnche pardoner? Wolde the chirche buy that?'

'Ylle handelle the chirche, Geoffrey. You juste gimme rawnche. What about a Wyfe in there, too?'

'A Wyfe?'

'Yeah. A Wyfe in a batthe.'

'Ylle givve it a trye, bosse,' saith I, notte havynge much altrenatyve, reale.

'Colde you lette me have oon firste drafte by Wednesday weke?' demandeth he.

Shitte, shitte, shitte.

The marketplace

Selling a work of art is much the same as selling double glazing or time-share, except the artist has to be more ruthless. It's no good sitting back and waiting for that lucky break or for fame to engulf you. To be a genius takes vigorous self-promotion, and that means Personal Motivation.

Schubert's lucky break: buried next to **Beethoven**

As Virginia Woolf said, 'If you've got it, flaunt it.' And she should have known. At her Thursday night Bloomsbury Assertiveness Training Workshops she would launch lethal salvoes of multi-headed, delayed action, smart put-downs at assembled guests, subjecting them to humiliating general knowledge quizzes and dousing them with buckets of pink slime.

'Thanks to Ginny,' recalls Vanessa Bell in her autobiography, *Sixty Years in a Deck-Chair*, 'we became immune to all forms of criticism, even though our work was crap.' With her cruel mental aerobics, Woolf transformed Lytton Strachey, 'that pale embroiderer of other people's lives' into the cigar-chomping, whisky-swigging author of the lurid *Elizabeth and Essex*, who left to tour America playing bottleneck guitar and run bootleg liquor before losing a duel in an El Paso bordello in 1932. Ginny had less success with Maynard Keynes, who couldn't hack it and gave up a promising career as a Dadaist performance poet to become an Independent Financial Advisor.

So take a lesson from Ginny's book – and I don't mean change sex half-way through the millennium. Say goodbye to that mumbling, diffident, aesthetic persona and learn to be aggressive, uncompromising, radical and shamelessly egotistical. And when you've learned to believe in yourself, let other people know it. Be seen around town. Turn up at every private view, book launch and first night. Remember, it's tough out there, so don't be put off. If asked, say, 'I'm with Melvyn.' Be prepared. Leave suddenly in mid-conversation. Before long you will be tagged as an unpredictable desperado of the art world and be invited to appear on *Midweek* with Libby Purves. Wherever you are, refuse to talk about your actual *œuvre*, insisting that, 'if I could talk about it, I wouldn't have to do it,' and that 'the

Talent spotter **Ben Nicholson** (*right*) does a deal
with Cornish painter **Alfred Wallis**

work should speak for itself'. American abstract painters were skilful exponents of the non-interview, either being involved in the creation of non-painting, or too drunk to talk properly, or both.

Another technique is to learn to hate the buyer as much as you hate yourself. Rothko, a Scorpio, always haggled with collectors, arguing, 'Look it's my misery I have to paint this stuff: it's your misery you have to love it. The price of this misery is $13,500.' He often destroyed the paintings after he'd sold them, thus, by some little-known rule of art economics, quadrupling their value. Likewise Kostabi regarded his customers as 'scum' – 'the more I spit in their faces, the more they beg me to sell.' This is a fine technique as long as you drink plenty of fluids.

The opposite of this technique is Uriah Heep humility. E. M. Forster used to tell everyone he met that he 'warmed both hands on the fire of life'. People would usually smile politely and pretend they'd left some ice-cream in the airing cupboard at home.

The most important lesson to remember is that you are selling not the product, but the lifestyle. Think of Jean Genet. When he took a meeting with a theatre manager did he have a product list packed with boulevard comedies guaranteed to put bums on seats? No. He had a product that was dredged from the gutter, full of searing questions about sexual identity, social control and the very dichotomy between illusion and reality itself. He put down his success to the three 'P's.

Preparation: his scripts were always professionally typed and bound, his market research was thorough, his graphics clear and he often used state-of-the-art multi-screen audio/visual packages to really hit that message home.

Personal presentation: shoe-polish is cheap, a smile costs nothing, there's no need to be a fop, but take it from Jean, neat appearance can be your biggest asset when closing a sale.

Psychopathic episodes: a signature on that contract, however shaky, is still a signature.

From rags to riches: **Jean Genet** wins the coveted Prix Goncourt award in 1948

William Butler Yeats, on the other hand, rarely took meetings, believing instead in the philosophy of 'making the customer come to you'. Using one of the many mailing lists he'd acquired from Ezra Pound, he'd send out a circular letter:

```
Dear Sir/Madam,
I am delighted to inform you that you've already won one
of the following prizes:
        A Model 'A' Ford
        A holiday for two where dips the rocky highland of
          Sleuth Wood in the lake
        A Kodak Camera outfit
        An 'I ♥ Roger Casement' T-shirt
All you have to do to claim your prize is come, bringing
this letter with you, to the Tower at Ballylea at 3.15 next
Monday.  I look forward to seeing you there.
        Congratulations!
        W.B.Yeats
```

Once he had assembled a sizeable crowd in the Tower, he'd lock the doors, chain up the toilets and start reciting. After the fourth or fifth reading of 'Cuchulain's Fight For The Sea', the people would buy anything, just to get out. Did that man shift books!

Many artists, including Walt Whitman and Joe Orton, have written pseudonymous letters to newspapers praising (or in Orton's case condemning) their own work. TV advertising of works of art is normally considered counter-productive since the gains accrued in publicity are more than outweighed by the loss of dignity and exclusivity – both key factors in the 'added value' which distinguishes a Great Work of Genius from 'Sensual Sensations, 20 Top Love Tracks of the Eighties'. These are, however, tough times for broadcasters. The going rate to buy yourself a major profile on the *South Bank Show* can be as little as fifty notes. No names, no pack drill.

The critics

Critics enjoy artist-baiting as a kind of blood sport. With barbed metaphor and verbal venom, they goad and prick their hapless quarries into frenzies of paranoia, until, intoxicated by the sulphurous vapours fuming from their cauldrons of manufactured cynicism, they deliver their *coups de grâce* in ferocious ejaculations of vitriol, fax their copy, and expire in paroxysms of genial self-regard. Sometimes they say nice things too.

There are two ways to deal with critics: either ignore them, or give as good as you get. In 1922, spotting James Joyce signing copies of *Ulysses* in her local Waterstone's, Virginia Woolf lowered her cab window and yelled, 'Don't buy it, folks – it's the work of a queasy undergraduate scratching his pimples!' to which Joyce retorted, quick as a flash, 'Rather a dick with acne than a dyke in a Hackney!' Ha ha ha. The things they say.

Willem and **Elaine de Kooning** forging Turner landscapes during the cold winter of '47: 'We had to eat'

James Joyce gets the idea for *Ulysses*

Cowboy songster **Tex Ritter** serves a plagiarism writ on composer **Aaron Copland,** Appalachian Mountains, spring 1944

D. H. Lawrence, also crossed off the Bloomsbury guest list for being rude, had little time for critics of his work, describing them as 'snivelling, dribbling, dithering, palsied, pulseless, slimy, belly-wriggling invertebrates', which was of course true, but they couldn't help it. 'They've got white of egg in their veins and their spunk is that watery, it's a marvel they can breed. The gibberers! God, how I hate them!' 'Never mind, our Dave,' his mother replied, as D.H. gnawed the worn, slack-blackened, knotted-rag hearthrug, 'put your trousers on and drink your Barley Cup. Forest are playing Sheffield Wednesday on t'wireless tonight.'

The important thing is not to take it at all personally. Shakespeare didn't sulk when the *Stratford Herald* slammed the ending of *Romeo and Juliet* as 'Colonel Mustard, in the library, with the spanner', he just nutted the bastard and got on with *Richard II*.

Remember, too, that although good publicity is better than bad, bad publicity is better than selling loft insulation systems. Bad reviews could mean you're ahead of your time; shunned by the Academy, you could attract a cult following and wear black a lot. Or they could mean you're rubbish.

Exercises

a Stand in front of a mirror and practise
 (i) the blag,
 (ii) the soundbyte,
 (iii) the face-to-face with Jeremy Isaacs pithy pause.
b Using a chicken breast (unfrozen), practise clawing your way to fame. (False fingernails may help.)
c Go to bed. Become an overnight sensation. (You have twelve hours.)

Ahead of their time: the original window designs for Chartres Cathedral, thirteenth century. 'Not spiritual enough,' said critics

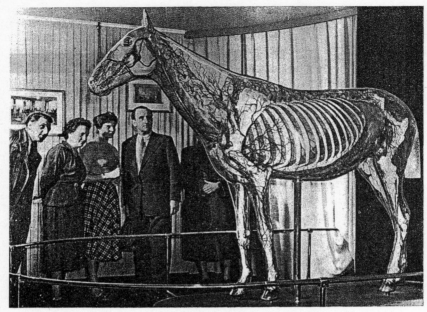

Visions of the future: sculptor **Damien Hirst** (*above*) explains his *We Are All Winners In The Race To The Glue Factory* to a group of Birmingham art lovers, whilst madcap video pioneer **Bill Viola** (*below*) sets up a multi-media installation at the 1994 Venice Biennale

15 Art – the final frontier

If Winter comes, can Spring be far behind, Rhett?

P. B. Shelley, 'Gone With the West Wind'

Returning from the opening night of a Joseph Beuys exhibition in 1966, Frankfurt Institute Professor Theodor Adorno, who had spent his life trying to avoid using the wrong words to describe what could not be described, shared a cab with Japanese art expert and ex-kamikazi pilot Mr Kevin Toyota.

'A work of art is always simultaneously itself and something other than itself,' said Adorno, making polite conversation. 'This otherness can lead astray: the moment you try to separate the meta-aesthetic aspect from art and hold it in your hand in all its purity, it evaporates.'

'Don't worry,' replied Kevin, 'it's only money.'

'But – what about genius?' asked the professor. 'Genius has no price tag.'

Mr Toyota was unmoved. 'In Japan we have a saying,' he said. 'The snowflake is not a butterfly, but neither of them stands much chance in a volcano.'

Adorno leaned forward and, tapping the driver on the shoulder, he said, 'Drop me off at the lights. The guy's nuts.'

Sixty years a dental technician, five years a sculptor. Seen alongside his installation, *Choppers*, is the surprise winner of this year's Turner Prize, **Mr Derek Hargreaves**

Luciano Berio – *bête noir* or *cordon bleu*?

The Good Genius Guide

compiled by Caroline Stafford

The ratings given below are statistically calculated according to the Moran™ Index of Genius Parameters. Information on aspects of achievement and lifestyle of all the major geniuses (the only precondition being that they are dead and mentioned in *Fortune* magazine's top 100,000 geniuses of all time) is input to a computer which then, according to the Index program, awards points for achievement in each category: under Nationality, for example 0 for Canadian, 10 for Russian; under Mental Health, 0 for being allowed out without supervision, 10 for chewing carpets; and so on throughout 3,048 separate categories. The numbers are crunched and a final rating allotted to each genius.

Below are the top 100, arranged alphabetically, with brief notes on their highest scoring attainments. The authors and publishers would like to make it clear that this choice is entirely statistical – no subjective judgement is involved. Thus while some may be alarmed at the inclusion, for example, of Jimi Hendrix, to the exclusion of William Shakespeare, they should blame Shakespeare for having had such a dull life and address all complaints to IBM.

> **KEY**
> * - overall rating
> n - nationality
> i - interesting disease(s)
> d - died young
> + - amusing or original death
> s - success in own lifetime & non-genius occupations
> m - mental health
> a - addiction to drugs/alcohol
> ! - depressing, shocking or incomprehensible
> qualities of work
> p - police record/interesting political, religious or
> philosophical affiliations
> x - sexual orientation/peccadilloes
> w - WOW factor, based on Hollywood biopics, *Arena* or
> *South Bank Show* retrospectives, devotional songs,
> sales of posters, T-shirts, postcards, badges etc.

** **Guillaume Apollinaire** (1880–1918) n - French/Polish; i - war wounds; d - 38. Misc. - coined the term 'Surrealism'. Buried in world's coolest graveyard, Père Lachaise cemetery, same as Oscar Wilde and Jim Morrison.

*** **Johann Sebastian Bach** (1685–1750) n - German; i - apoplexy; x - 20 children; w - Hamlet adverts, Swingle Singers.

* **Roger Bacon** (1214–92) n - English; + - shortly after publishing a treatise on warding off the infirmities of old age; p - hated by Franciscans, imprisoned for 'suspected novelties' for 15 years, meddler in the black arts; w - often referred to as 'Dr Mirabilis'.

**** **Charles Baudelaire** (1821–67) n - French; a - opium addict, alcoholic; p - Satanist, sided with revolutionaries of 1848 in spite of being an aristocrat, prosecuted for impropriety in 1864; x - general perverting around.

** **Aubrey Beardsley** (1872–98) n - English; i - consumption; d - 25; m - miserable bugger, pornographer, big nose; p - co-founder of the 'Decadents'.

*** **Samuel Beckett** (1906–89) n - Irish; s - Nobel Prize for literature 1969; m - miserable bugger; ! - the bankruptcy of the human spirit was his stock in trade.

*** **Ludwig van Beethoven** (1770–1827) n - German; i - deaf, repulsive appearance, pock-faced, excessively hairy; m - didn't wash, shocking table manners; w - the stormtrooper of Romanticism, wrote incidental music for *A Clockwork Orange*. Misc. - father tried to pre-date his birth so he could be an infant prodigy.

*** **Brendan Behan** (1923–64) n - Irish; d - 41; a - alcoholic, whiskey/stout; p - 14 years for trying to blow up a shipyard as a member of the IRA; x - pimp in Paris, jumped anything moving; w - wrote lyrics for *The Auld Triangle* by the Pogues.

* **Bix Beiderbecke** (1903–31) n - American; d - 28; a - born drunk, died drunk, smiled drunk, dressed drunk; w - book and film, *Young Man With A Horn* and James Bolam.

*** **William Blake** (1757–1827) n - English; m - oh, please!; ! - believed he was guided by perpetual visitations from the spirit world; p - cloud cuckoo land; w - postcards in student shops.

** **Hieronymus Bosch** (1450–1516) n - Dutch; m - standard Catholic loony; p - posthumously accused of heresy; w - the Surrealists claimed him as their own.

* **Bertolt Brecht** (1898–1956) n - German; p - fled Hitler because of Communism, straight into the arms of US Un-American Activities Committee.

* **Anne Brontë** (1820–49) n - English; d - 29. Misc. - the least known of the three sisters, and the one who died youngest, therefore makes the grade.

* **Rupert Brooke** (1887–1915) n - English; d - 28; x - WW1; w - dull poetry, but jolly good-looking.

* **Elizabeth Barrett Browning** (1806–61) n - English; i - injured spine while saddling pony; m - psychotic hairdo. Misc. - eloped with Robert Browning.

* **Diderik Buxtehude** (1637–1707) n - Danish; s - Bach walked 200 miles from Germany to hear him play. Misc. - crazy guy, crazy name!

***** **George Gordon Lord Byron** (1788–1824) n - English; i - club-foot; d - 36; x - marsh-fever at Missolonghi; s - the ABBA of his day; m - mad, bad and dangerous to know; a - laudanum/claret/brandy, you name it; ! - occasionally escaped from fantasy back into reality; p - supported anything uppity; x - slept with his sister, and probably your sister; w - WOW!

* **John Cage** (1912–93) n - American; m - does things with rubber bands; ! - !; p - Buddhist. Misc. - one of the world's leading experts on edible fungi.

** **Albert Camus** (1913–60) n - French; i - sickly; + - car smash; s - Nobel Prize 1957; m - a bit touchy; p - edited *Combat* with Sartre, Existentialist who reformed after he got fed up with being miserable; w - professional footballer.

Elizabeth Barrett: from couch potato to gravy with Browning

** **Benvenuto Cellini** (1500–71) n - Italian; s - achieved through the murder of most of his rivals; m - psychopath; p - slagged off the artistic tastes of Popes; w - rakish autobiography.

** **Frédéric Chopin** (1810–49) n - Polish; i - coughed a lot; d - 39; + - consumption; m - dated a lady with a bloke's name.

* **Jean Cocteau** (1889–1963) n - French; a - opium; ! - weird and dirty; p - converted to Catholicism by Jacques Maritain; x - weird and dirty; w - great profile.

*** **Samuel Taylor Coleridge** (1772–1834) n - English; m - carpet-chewing, wrote 'Ode to Dejection'; a - opium/claret/brandy; ! - have you read 'The Ancient Mariner'?

* **Richard Dadd** (1818–87) n - English; m - spent 40 years in Bedlam and Broadmoor; ! - liked painting little fairies; p - murdered his father.

* Salvador Dali (1904–89) n – Spanish; s – huge; m, – liked to wear a diving suit around the house; ! – referred to his works as 'hand-painted dream photographs'.

** Dante Alighieri (1265–1321) n – Italian; s – backed a few losers and got exiled; m – morbid fixation with Hell, fell in love aged 9 with somebody he never spoke to and never got over it; p – fought against the Ghibellines, only they never noticed; x – fell in love aged 9 with somebody he never spoke to and never got over it.

*** Fyodor Dostoevsky (1821–81) n – Russian; m – morbid, woeful, miserable, anguished; p – condemned to death for revolutionary activities (later commuted to hard labour in Siberia).

** T. S. Eliot (1888–1965) n – American/British; i – terrible cough; m – wore green make-up but had his wife committed; ! – in spades; x – banker; w – wrote *Cats*.

** F. Scott Fitzgerald (1896–1940) n – American; i – consumptive; d – 44; s – bestseller at 23, but never out of debt for rest of life; m – married a barmcake; a – alcoholic; w – *The Great Gatsby*, therefore indirectly responsible for interior décor of many wine-bars.

*** Paul Gauguin (1848–1903) n – French; s – lived in a hut; m – gave up successful career in banking; x – Tahitians; w – lived with Van Gogh.

** Jean Genet (1911–86) n – French; m – space case; a – loads; ! – absurd reflections on ritual, dream and fantasy; p – thief, always in and out of prison; x – not like the home life of our own dear Queen Mother.

***** Vincent Van Gogh (1853–90) n – Dutch; d – 37; + – shot himself in a corn-field; s – loser; m – religious mania, self-mutilation and the rest; a – should have tried more, might have cheered him up; w – starry, starry night.

*** Ernest Hemingway (1899–1961) n – American; i – there is that thing about his *cojone(s)*; + – shot himself; s – Nobel Prize 1954; m – knew the pain that it is to be a man; a – he saw the drink. He drank the drink. It was a fine thing to drink the drink and feel its drinkiness inside you; x – he loved the big fish.

** Jimi Hendrix (1942–70) n – American; d – 28; + – inhaled vomit after barbiturate intoxication; s – made the cover of the *Rolling Stone*; a – everything, and a side order of the same again; x – everything, and a side order of the same again; w – made a lovely poster.

** Billie Holliday (1915–59) n – American; d – 44; + – OD; m – always chose the wrong man; a – the lot; p – horribly; w – Diana Ross.

*** Robert Johnson (1911–38) n – American; d – 27; + – poisoned by a jealous husband; s – sold soul to Devil but didn't collect; ! – violent but fair; x – lemon squeezing.

*** James Joyce (1882–1941) n – Irish; ! – riverrun, past Eve and Adam's, from swerve of shore to bend of bay, brings us by a commodius vicus of recirculation back to Howth Castle and Environs; p – widely banned in Britain, USA and Ireland.

*** Franz Kafka (1883–1924) n – Austrian; i – nasty cough; s – steady job in Workers' Accident Insurance Institution; m – hypersensitive, introspective, Oedipus complex, didn't play well with other children; ! – depressive, shocking and incomprehensible, so full marks there.

** John Keats (1795–1821) n – English; i – consumption; d – 26; a – laudanum.

Billie Holliday: loved entertaining

Jack Kerouac: crazy mixed-up guy, going nowhere fast

* Søren Kierkegaard (1813–55) n – Danish; m – unable to afford one of his own, he became obsessed by a mysterious guilt of his father's; ! – 'one ought to be a mystery, not only to others, but also to one's self ... Ah, such a dish of buckwheat porridge! I would give more than my birthright for it!'

*** D. H. Lawrence (1885–1930) n – English; i – consumption; d – 45; m – no sense of humour, married a German; p – prosecuted for obscenity in 1915; x – liked dirty words, gave his dick a silly name.

**** **John Lennon** (1940–80) n - English; d - 40; + - shot by fan; m - married Yoko; a - married Yoko; ! - married Yoko; p - married Yoko; x - married Yoko; w - Julian's dad.

** **Christopher Marlowe** (1564–93) n - English; d - 29; + - stabbed in the eye in Deptford; p - arrested for disseminating atheist opinions; x - walked on the Wild Side.

* **Vladimir Mayakovsky** (1893–1930) n - Russian; d - 37; + - topped himself; p - revolutionary mouthpiece of the Bolsheviks.

*** **Michelangelo Buonarroti** (1475–1564) n - Italian; s - gave good network; m - well, he did argue with the Pope; x - Larry Grayson fan.

** **Yukio Mishima** (1925–70) n - Japanese; i - delicate; d - 45; + - the best, had his friend behead him in front of the Commandant of the Eastern Army after delivering a speech; m - liked death; p - right-wing patriot.

*** **Amedeo Modigliani** (1884–1920) n - Italian; d - 35; m - one tube short of the full paintbox, threw girlfriends out of windows; a - hashish, ether, alcohol; p - his exhibition of 1918 closed for indecency on first day; x - seduced his housemaid before he was 16; w - postcard sales.

*** **Wolfgang Amadeus Mozart** (1756–91) n - Austrian; d - 35; x - typhus; s - good earner, but spendy-wendy wife; m - haunted by his Requiem Mass being his own; w - *Amadeus*, the film, the play, the album, the coffee mug.

** **Edvard Munch** (1863–1944) n - Norwegian; s - work caused uproar and was withdrawn from exhibition; m - dingaling about love and death; a - drink; ! - wanted to 'dissect souls'.

** **Friedrich Nietzsche** (1844–1900) n - German; m - said 'God is dead' then, later, believed himself to be God with the result that he spent the last 12 years of his life in an insane asylum.

* **Omar Khayyam** (c. 1050–1130) n - Persian; a - liked his flask of wine, his book of verse and his thou so much, he bought the company.

* **Joe Orton** (1933–67) n - English; d - 34; + - battered to death by lover; a - pills and booze; ! - complaints from Tunbridge Wells; p - defaced library books; x - liked nothing better than a classic, English cottage.

Orwell (Eric Blair): chronicler of adversity and brother of Lionel

*** **Charlie Parker** (1920–55) n - American; d - 35; a - enough horse to kill one; ! - accused of playing 'Chinese Music', developed jive talk to new, incomprehensible heights; p - various arrests for possession, relaxed at Camarillo; w - *Bird Lives*.

**** **Pablo Picasso** (1881–1973) n - Spanish; s - wasn't short of a few bob; ! - made a goat out of a wastepaper basket and so on, you know the sort of thing; p - investigated by both the FBI and the KGB; x - anything with a controlled body temperature; w - a whole week on BBC2.

** **Sylvia Plath** (1932–63) n - American; d - 30; + - gas oven; m - shock treatment and insulin therapy; x - married Ted Hughes.

Sylvia Plath: hated cooking

** **Edgar Allen Poe** (1809–49) n - American; d - 40; + - on a bender, days before his second wedding; m - lived in terror of his own suffocation; a - dipsomaniac; x - impotent, necrophiliac, married a 13-year-old; w - Hammer Horror.

* **Jackson Pollock** (1912–56) n - American; d - 44; + - auto accident; s - *Time* magazine called him 'Jack the dripper'; a - alcoholic.

** **Marcel Proust** (1871–1921) n - French; i - semi-invalid; m - social butterfly till his mother died when he was 34, after which he shut himself into a cork-lined room; ! - long; x - eerie.

** **Arthur Rimbaud** (1854–91) n - Belgian; i - leg amputated; d - 37; s - wrote best stuff between ages of 15 and 19; m - see Verlaine; a - opium, absinthe; w - often confused with Sylvester Stallone.

* **Henri Rousseau** (1844–1910) n - French; s - assistant customs officer, retired at 50; m - compulsive liar, nice but dim.

* **George Sand** (1804–76) n - French; m - had a bloke's name; w - see Chopin.

*** **Jean-Paul Sartre** (1905–80) n - French; m - grumpy at the best of times; ! - atheistic, Existentialist, obsessed with the nausea of existence; p - Communist; w - name is rhymed with Montmartre by Fred Astaire in *Funny Face*.